Advanced Primer of Sidereal Astrology

J. K. Goodwin

Kala Purusha Publications

Integrated
Occult
Studies

Integrated Occult Studies presents
<u>Advanced Primer of Sidereal Astrology</u>
Produced by Kala Purusha Publications

Second Edition 2009
limited printing

ISBN 978-144-860-869-0

Contact the author and astrologer:
J. K. Goodwin
375 S. Main, Suite #108
Moab, UT 84532
jerouldkielgoodwin@yahoo.com

Dedication

To all serious occultists and transcendentalists
Who, with courage, go against the mundane grain
Defying a world full of fanatics,
Who are covering almost everyone with their nescience

Table of contents

PREFACE

The diagram used Egyptian glyphs as symbols for the planets and signs of the zodiac. These symbols were within what I would come to know as the North Indian construct for displaying a chart: A diamond and an 'X' inside of a square. When I saw my first sidereal horoscope, drawn up by one budding young American astrologer, I was fascinated. Intuitively I knew, through an attracted intelligence brimming with realization, that there were many important secrets contained within it.

This was in the early spring of 1978; I was twenty-seven but had not really had, up to that point, any contact with either tropical or sidereal astrology. During the latter part of my aborted collegiate escapade six years earlier, I was heavy into symbolism and interpretations of what was the reality behind events I experienced. In terms of Ouspensky's classification, I would have then been labeled a number three making more or less wild stabs at trying to become a four—but without any specific knowledge that such was the case. Intellectual ascertainments and measurements were a priority to me, and they still are. This would later be verified astrologically: I have no planets in any of the water signs in my natal horoscope.

In the late Seventies, I had no hesitancy to immediately fly out to the West Coast and meet this occultist, the one who had created the abovementioned chart. He was also a member of the same cult as our mutual friend—for whom he had made that horoscope—and was almost exactly my same age. I soon sat down with him in his small, clean apartment in Los Angeles, and he was encouraged by my keen interest. This brand of mysticism was very suitable for both of us.

Then, I began to learn basics the long way, prior to word processors, computers, and instant charts. We had to do the math by hand in those days, as there were no software programs to assist in this calculation. With diligence, I learned how to calculate lagna (the ascendant) using an ephemeris, a daylight savings time manual, a book of the rising signs for different latitudes and longitudes, and deducting an ayanamsha. The ayanamsha he used was the Lahiri ayanamsha.

To my first teacher's credit, he did inform me that there was an ayanamsha controversy, and, in this book, you will overcome that limitation. It took me a long time to finally resolve it. Much of what I read back then—or was initially taught—turned out to be either flat out wrong or, at best, only a very imperfect application of sidereal laws and principles.

This treatise is a shortcut for you—and that principle is applied throughout my writings here. You get to take advantage of the difficult learning curve that I had to pass through for many decades. I had to figuratively crawl on glass in order to finally peel away so many contradictions and distortions covering the real system. However, in 1978, my enthusiasm for this occult science kept any long-term hesitancy completely at bay. Back then, it could not even germinate.

Not knowing how tough a road it was going to be can only now be considered a good thing. My naiveté of the lacunas in my first inculcations, looking back on it, also ultimately proved helpful. Actually, there was a very big astrological problem between my initial teacher and myself, and I do not think that he was aware of it then. There are twenty-seven lunar constellations, and twenty-six of them have a counterpart (amongst the other twenty-five) that is very inimical. This enmity is mutual.

I and this fellow astrologer had one of these sets, and we were destined to always work at cross-purposes whenever acting together on anything. It was a nasty, star-crossed situation, but, as Ringo sang (in a song actually written by George Harrison), "You know it don't come easy". Payment is a universal principle, and that was part of what I had to pay in order to earn the right to produce this book.

You do not have to learn how to calculate charts long-hand, unless you really want to do so. I do not teach that process in this book. Instead, I recommend that you purchase or secure a sidereal software program in order to have charts instantly calculated, with amenities. I am not going to recommend any specific company's program; that research is part of the project that you must take on for yourself. However, I am strongly recommending that you secure a software program that affords the facility to program in the ayanamsha of your choice—and not just from a limited set of ayanamshas offered. This is because, as indicated above, I am going to be giving you the correct ayanamsha, the one that actually works. None of the "standard issue" ayanamshas will do.

You must be able to set the parameters for this ayanamsha, and it's really not very difficult at all. The tropical positions, previous to deducting the ayanamsha, are ludicrous. The Fagan ayanamsha is way off; almost as bad is the Lahiri ayanamsha. Neither Krishnamur-

2

ti's nor Yuktesvara's is accurate, either. Raman's, although closer, is still not accurate enough. There is no need to waste a whole chapter in this book describing, in meticulous detail, how to calculate a chart long-hand. The overwhelming majority of people who buy a VCR never read the complicated instructions contained in the manual, listing all the detailed steps required for utilizing many features. Most of these owners rely on family and friends.

If I included all of the methodology for hand-calculated charts, how many of my readers would even bother with that chapter? Perhaps one in one hundred would do so. To repeat, get a sidereal program that allows you to create your own ayanamsha. As of 2009, we are still in the post-modern electronic age. So take advantage of those amenities while they are not only still available but also offer so many other advantages.

I concentrated on my own chart in the early years, and that's the best strategy for learning the science. Trying to figure out your scheduled karmas is not as important as trying to understand your nature. At the time of first breath, the planets stamp the astral body with the impressions of its essential characteristics; this is what you should now concentrate upon in the rudimentary stage of the study.

Immediate karmas are determined by daily lunar movements through the nakshatras or constellations. These can, in most cases, be either totally or partially overcome—if you are aware of them and act accordingly. At times, you must know how to dovetail them.

Now, transits are more difficult to transcend. Much harder to transcend than transits are the scheduled effects of the dashas or major life stages. These, as I shall subsequently reveal to you, are thoroughly misunderstood by practically the whole sector of Western siderealists. Indeed, as of 2009, only one sidereal software program that I am aware of even (and that imperfectly) calculates the pindayu, nisargayu, and amshayu methods. This dasha system indicates destiny—and destiny is difficult to overcome. Indeed, when fate is transcended, it can only be replaced by Providence; we have a very limited range of independence, ultimately. Knowing the actual dasha working at any given time is helpful in the matter of overcoming or psychologically accepting its influence.

In December of 1979, I was undergoing an excruciating transition, this time in a northwest suburb of Portland called Beaverton. Another intrigue had been laid on me, and I was at a crossroads. I had pretty much neglected astrology at that time. While browsing through a small bookstore in the downtown Portland area, I "coincidentally" stumbled upon a small book of knowledge from India, entitled Muhurtha.

The author of this bright yellow paperback was the reputed siderealist B. V Raman, who I had briefly met in Bangalore earlier that year. I had met him on an amavasya (new Moon day), but he said that meeting people who were in a renounced lifestyle was favorable on that tithi. The English in his book, as well as the syntax, was haphazard. Nevertheless, it was still eminently readable. I don't remember what I paid for it, but, whatever the amount was, I have recouped that investment many thousands of times over.

A muhurtha, sometimes translated as "a moment," is a subdivision of time. In Hindi, we often find the term ghati. The ghati, on the equinox day when sunlight and darkness are of equal lengths, is measured equally throughout the twenty-four hours. A muhurtha consists of two ghatis. Calculating the muhurtha for a given event or initiative is important, because some of these moments are auspicious and some are inauspicious.

This Muhurtha book provided details about election astrology, much of which will be passed on to you (but in a more organized format) in a later chapter of this book. Discovering Muhurtha constituted a colossal psychological breakthrough for me.

The former leader of our group had given us an indirect ultimatum from afar; the handful of men still in Oregon with me now looked for new leadership. If we made a drastic move and it proved a failure, they would abandon my direction and association. I did not want to capitulate to the ultimatum, but I was also unprepared, at that time, to go it alone.

I considered the Muhurtha book as a godsend. In December, we all decided to leave the now shivering Pacific Northwest and travel to sunny and much warmer Florida. However, this long trip was fraught with potential pitfalls, even up to the point of disaster.

I worked long and hard—by hand, of course—to try to come up with the best lagna (ascendant) possible, utilizing all the knowledge in this handbook of election astrology. It was all very new to me, and it was cumbersome work. Finally, I arrived at something (a day and time) that did not get nipped by one of so many hidden traps or forbidden times detailed in the book (and I had not nearly discovered all of them at that time).

The bags left the doorway for the vehicle at the moment when the auspicious time arrived. The trip went surprisingly smooth and even included an unexpected and successful visit with my Mother on the way. We also had no difficulty finding two excellent accommodations in Tampa, as well as income sources more or less immediately upon arrival. I attributed these successes, in no small part, to that election calculation. I hit a good vein on the first try, but, about one and one-half years later, I would calculate what I thought was a very good election chart for our initial land purchase. However, I did not notice nakshatra gandanthara, mentioned in only one place in Muhurtha. This purchase led to a big loss, because, at least in part, that evil conjunction spoiled all the other configurations which appeared to be set for prosperity.

Do not expect footnotes, a glossary, an index, and all the other so-called professional trappings; I simply do not write in that way. Neither were any of the original Vedic literatures compiled like that. This does not mean that I am against the Western style of professional writing; I utilize it when I read books, but I do not employ it in all of my writings. They are valuable for their content, because they are clear and concise. The quotes from Swami Vijnanananda are per his 1912 original work entitled Brihaj-jatakam of Varaha Mihira, New Delhi, India: Oriental Books Reprint Corp. If you are an academic requiring that all books you accept be perfect in terms of the contemporary standard, then you will probably be unable to appreciate what I have to offer you here in this advanced primer.

The best way to read my book is to flush out all that you think that you know on the topic I am elucidating, wipe a clean slate, and more or less start anew with sidereal astrology as it is. This means that you must first discover and then deliberate on the qualities and characteristics of your own chart, as aforementioned. You need to know it backwards and forwards, inside and out. You need to see where you are really at, what is your foundational temperament and attitude, and how you can get the most from your personal (but conditioned) self, i.e., the process of metaphysical and spiritual upgrading and progressive occult development.

All the seeds you need to grow a forest of personal sidereal success are contained in this book, along with some subsidiary knowledge. That is how I define the second octave of this process, according to scale. The method entails diagnosing potentials, preventing looming problems from developing, and prescribing appropriate methods and remedies—in terms of occult knowledge through core sidereal astrology. Radical means root, and this book gets to the core or the root of this science.

In some places in it, I'll provide personal notes or anecdotes. Sometimes the presentation is a bit unorthodox. Despite that, the knowledge is presented authoritatively from higher Vedic mind.

OM TAT SAT
J. K. GOODWIN, Sept. 5, 2008

INTRODUCTION

It is a question of valuation. For all progressive occultists who actually require understanding their horoscopes in terms of sidereal astrology, the knowledge has now been presented in a new and improved format. For most of the Western world, the science more or less remains lost in antiquity due to a great deal of adulteration.

Tropical astrology is nothing more than a twist-upon-a-twist derivation from an original Vedic paradigm—and a subdivision at that—known as the tajjika system. The tajjika system is employed in the varshaphala interpretation of Vedic charts, i.e., the annual solar return chart. The emphasis in this system is interpretation via applying and separating aspects and conjunctions. Western astrology can give some relevant and even valuable advice when it comes to interpretation of transits and angular relationships between and amongst the planets. Its planetary sign placements are almost completely illusory, and that is not helpful.

The tropical zodiac is nothing more than an imposition that only partially overlaps the real signs of the sidereal zodiac. Tropical astrology, on average, places a planet in the wrong sign three-quarters of the time. In terms of the smaller subdivisions of the sign, i.e., the navamsha, trimsamsha, and dvadasamsha, the Western positions cannot yield accurate results.

Just as importantly, tropical astrology is loaded with concoctions. When it assigns lordships of signs to Uranus, Neptune, and Pluto, it deviates from the astro-reality; these three far-flung planets (two of which are rather small orbs, and the other smaller than Jupiter or Saturn) have no influence on human affairs. When it ignores the semi-invisible upagrahas (sub-planets) of Rahu and Ketu (the north and south lunar nodes) as nothing more than mathematical points on the ecliptic, some interpretations and yogas are lost in the process. However, from my experience, the seven major planets are far more important than are Rahu and Ketu. Varahamihira in his <u>Brihaj-jataka</u> indirectly verifies this by barely mentioning them at all.

Focusing on the misunderstandings of tropical astrology is ultimately a diversionary engagement. The real issues must be confronted. They all are directly related to sidereal astrology, or, rather, to wrong schools of thought and interpretation that are being passed off in the West today as sidereal astrology. Eastern astrology is a treasure house for any serious occultist or transcendentalist. In order to open that and take full advantage of its intellectual and practical riches, a solid basis of knowledge and real understanding is the first requirement.

The Vedas are ultra-extensive compendiums of knowledge. In and of themselves, they are mostly incomprehensible to the vast majority of the world. There are six separate subdivisions of the Vedas that are, although difficult, not as remote of access: One of these is called Jyotish. Sidereal astrology is derived from it. Seers of the Truth, through enlightened consciousness, made commentaries throughout the millennia on this Eye of the Vedas. These seers, also sometimes called rishis, were for the most part domiciled in the Indian subcontinent.

In what can, from one perspective, be called *relatively* recent times (this Earth and human societies have been in existence for many millions of years), the science of sidereal astrology spread from India to China, Chaldea, Mesopotamia, and a little after that, to Egypt. These other cultures were originally breakaway Vedic cultures. After that, it spread from there to other such cultures, the Greeks, and then, obviously, to the Roman Empire. With some Middle Eastern influence, the Hellenic and Roman remnants of this science made their way into Europe during the Dark Ages; they began to be better received during later Medieval times. They were completely converted to tropical astrology during this transition, however, although that deviation commenced before their spread into Northern Europe. By the Gothic epoch and with the Renaissance in full bloom, all European astrologers were believers in tropical astrology; it is doubtful that any of them even knew about the sidereal system at that time.

As the science spread out from India, each culture that adopted it amongst its intelligentsia distorted and dumbed it down. Unfortunately, this is an inevitable devolutionary process in this age; a descending octave. When advanced metaphysical or occult knowledge contacts the astral environment of untrained people, it must become warped to some degree.

Of the many myths surrounding this science, a particularly Western egocentric one is most odious. This is the scholarly propaganda that Indian or sidereal astrology is an import from Ptolemaic Greek astrology. Nothing could be further from the truth. Back in those days, both commerce and occult thought were often exchanged between sages of the Asian subcontinent and its Mediterranean counterpart. Ptolemy learned his astronomy (and the astrology based upon it) from Eastern sources, not vice-versa. What he did with it after that is anybody's guess.

Astrology is an occult science, because it completely depends upon subtle or hidden principles. Even conceding or recognizing the existence of these realities requires a different kind of thinking (Ouspensky called it philosophical thinking). This thinking is highly intuitive; when fixed in sankhya yoga, it becomes clear and free from contradiction.

One of the well-known aphorisms of this thought is: "As above, so below." This indicates both an intuitive and a rational principle. When a certain alignment is present in the higher spheres of the universe (macrocosm), i.e., in the planets and constellations, the manifestation of that alignment, its effect, is also then present in the microcosm of any event or entity born at that time. Each human being represents the energy of the stellar alignment that was present "in the heavens" at that moment.

There is another equally important principle of metaphysical thinking connected to sidereal astrology, viz., laws are operative in these aforementioned alignments. By consulting true sidereal or astrological teachings, and by accurately determining the motions, placements, and interrelationships of the planets and the constellations (as well as the ascendant), we can *apply* these laws to advantage. Or, put in another way, we can act or not act in such a way as to have the planetary juxtapositions either be entirely harmonious with us, mostly helpful, or not as harmful (as they otherwise would be if we were ignorant of these higher laws). Things fall into place once we comprehend and act upon this principle.

A human being, unless advanced transcendentally, is completely controlled by the effects of his previously-generated karma; sometimes it is instant karma. Still, he also often has a measure of freedom to generate new actions. If these actions are karmic, mixed karmic, or vikarmic (bad karma) in nature, such causes will produce their effects in due course of time. If he or she can utilize sidereal knowledge after having received it, life will proceed downstream in a smoother way than otherwise.

There will be less failure, because a man will know his limitations. There will be significant successes with what only appears to be middling effort expended, because a man will understand his strengths. Finally, a man of sidereal knowledge will know where to invest the required effort that can produce a successful result, because he will better understand the laws that are operative in the process as a whole. At best, knowledge of sidereal astrology is a powerful tool in any transcendentalist's arsenal for fighting the illusory energy. At the very least, this knowledge represents good karma for the person receiving it, with attendant side effects.

Our sidereal horoscope indicates our past karma, current qualities in relation to the modes of nature, and our best courses of action. It can also be used, in a subsidiary manner, in order to know how to gain knowledge of liberation from the repetitive cycle of birth and death, i.e., reincarnation.

Varahamihira was arguably the greatest sidereal astrologer of post-Vedic times. His chief astrological treatise is the Brihaj-jataka. Some centuries ago, an astrologer named Bhatta Utpaala compiled a commentary on this work. At the turn of the Twentieth Century, Swami Vijnanananda of Belur Math in India translated the work into English with his own additional commentary. Our treatise is based upon all this previous effort by very knowledgeable men in the science.

Sidereal astrology has been hidden for a long time; for all practical purposes, as far as the West is concerned, it has *only* been covered. Being covered, however, does not mean that it has been destroyed. It cannot be destroyed, and now it is becoming uncovered. The quasi-truths and pseudo-principles of today's popularized versions of sidereal astrology (Western sidereal astrology, so to speak) will react by either ignoring this treatise or resisting the knowledge. As such, it will require some courage on your part to take advantage of this book. You also have to possess the mental and intellectual capacity required in order to comprehend its teachings.

Although there are solid arguments in favor of the idea that sidereal astrology is a science of predestination, this is not a cent-per-cent truth. If you uproot a specific nescience (avidya), you uproot a cause. As such, there is no longer really a karmic requirement for the scheduled effect, because the lesson to be gained by the reaction has already been assimilated. We generally walk right into our bad karmic reactions; we set ourselves up for them. However, there is no need to do this. If the universal controllers still insist upon dealing out a token punishment, then that mitigation can also be attributed to our astrological enlightenment. As we all know, more knowledge general-ly means less misfortune.

Everything is embedded within the creative, maintaining, and destructive forces of the Universal Form. *Source* Universal is represented by the planets and the constellations. Kala means time. The sidereal science can be called the science of time. There is a kind of cosmic determinism, but most human beings conversely are under the illusion that they have the power to do, that they are entirely free agents. Sidereal astrology, combined with transcendental knowledge, is a complete system that eradicates this illusion right from the gate.

We live in a cosmic ocean of planetary and stellar vibrations. Astrological influences also pervade gross matter, however the radia-tions we speak of here are mostly of the nature of astral vibrations or impressions. The aforementioned rishis realized just how the astro-realities worked and produced formulas accordingly. These formulas, in conjunction with time, constitute the basic principles of sidereal astrology. For example, in election astrology (arguably the most im-portant sector of the science), you want to initiate your action at a time when the planetary vibrations (astral influences) are most propitious. This means you attempt to harmonize the macrocosm in relation to your natal chart via astrological laws operating in connection to the nature of the effort itself.

The personal horoscope indicates the past karma, the results to be expected, and the nature of the conditioned soul who was born at that moment. It is like a concise message encoded in planetary glyphs and similar symbols. The chart appears to be technical, but the realiza-tions you can glean from it are not. We have all heard the aphorism that knowledge is power. In the case of sidereal knowledge, that pow-er can be developed by studying the diagnosis of a natal chart and then applying either proscriptive or preventative initiatives in accor-dance with corresponding vibrations or influences on the astral plane. This constitutes a dynamic process.

To some extent, Carl Jung introduced sidereal astrology to the West when he pontificated that whatever is done at a given moment, or whoever is born at a given time, has the qualities of that vibration present in the heavens at that moment. These planetary and stellar radiations or vibrations are incessantly pouring down upon the Earth from different regions of the universe. Some are heavenly and some are hellish, as on all levels of the universe (upper, middle, and lower) heavenly, middle, and hellish planets exist. These radiations emanate

11

from what only appears to be vacant outer space. They continuously affect our mind, our intelligence, our false ego, and our consciousness in general.

We feel harmony when they match our expectations in the manifest world; we are then happy. When they serve to impede our efforts, they also reinforce our distress. We can know these vibrations, their sources, their Ultimate Source, and we can move in tune with them even when we don't particularly like the song they are playing. *Source* Universal is constantly engaged in His pastime with us, and He does have a playful, albeit sometimes mischievous, side to Him.

The sidereal zodiac will increasingly be recognized as the band of signs that it actually is. It is called the fixed zodiac. In due course, even in the West, that will be recognized as truth and the way to necessarily determine the real positions of the planets. There is an astral connection between and amongst the two upa-grahas, the stellar zodiac, and the seven major planets of antiquity. Distance is a factor in relation to their vibrations reaching and affecting man. Saturn is a huge planet and close enough to us for its vibrations to land on human beings with significant effect.

The absurd materialism and voidism of the agnostic post-modern scientists—and their collusion with the military-industrial-political complex—cannot keep the sidereal science down forever; Truth always triumphs eventually. Satyam eva jayate. The sidereal science is not a mere belief system. These varying influences are always manifesting their energetic representations in the visible world. Any intelligent man or woman can very soon attain the eyes to see how this is going on. There is no need to dismiss any of it with a self-serving rationalization that the teaching is only speculative.

This book is being presented in concentrated and practical terms; it is not simply a catalog of interesting ideas. Sidereal astrology reveals to us the background or hidden truth, a *unified* template in the material *universe*, in which various forces are at play in all fields of endeavor at all times. Every other science should utilize this one in order to perfect its field of activity. The chart spells out the language of the cosmos. Sidereal astrology is operative in every dimension of life—and that means in all the affairs of common, mundane activities, as well.

Currently, in the post-modern West, all of its cultures are founded upon democratic and capitalistic cornerstones, not on occult or spiritual foundations. Sidereal astrology, therefore, is not part of any Western foundation. Ouspensky would call current Western influences part of mechanical forces, which seek to destroy, suppress, divert, or cover genuine occult influences. As individuals moving against the grain of these forces, practitioners of sidereal astrology need to weave it into the fabric of their *own* personal and cultural development. It must serve as a personal psychological cornerstone; it can be upgraded when buddhi-yoga is activated. We can help our social circle by using sidereal merit; practitioners of this science cannot be mundane contrarians.

The science of the post-modern world is not integrated with reality. The democratic/capitalist culture does not know how to take advantage of sidereal influences that are nevertheless present at all times and at all levels. Because the culture at large is either skeptical of, or cynical about, such hidden sidereal impressions, almost every Westerner is involved in analyzing everything to death. We are all instead supposed to be developing a holistic approach or synthesis to life, seeing pantheistic, pan-entheistic, henotheistic, and ultimately theistic influences. True theism must be integrated with sidereal astrology in order to have a solid footing in any progressive culture, and the time has come to recognize this.

For the Golden Age to dawn worldwide, it must first manifest on a cultural level in the West, because this culture currently controls the rest of the world. Its economic and military networks cast a predominating shadow over every other civilization. Sidereal astrology was once an integral part of many great empires. It can be rejuvenated again to serve mankind in an even more potent way—but only if the West accepts it.

Because the current culture either does not know of it or rejects it, Western astrological science has now degraded into little more than a mass of cosmic superstitions rooted in various inanities or fortune telling. Worse yet, popular sidereal astrology in the West embraces a number of shibboleths. These have been mindlessly accepted without any overarching cultural resistance to their false premises. Rejuvenating the genuine science of sidereal astrology is therefore important. If enough Westerners become seriously aware of it, the devolutionary momentum can be checked and reversed. Knowledge of the real science can one day be available for mainstream applications if the current momentum changes.

Embedded within the structure of things are the laws of sidereal astrology. The planets channel various influences, and, as time moves, these impressions change in both course and intensity. We live in a cosmos governed by time and planetary influences. As Jung said, every moment in time is of a certain intensity and quality. These astrological forces produce fields of karma here on Earth. We can determine both the quality (guna) and scheduled action or reaction (karma) of our current incarnation by understanding the symbolic synchronicity of the horoscope in accordance with the laws of time.

Destiny is determined by decisions and actions. How can we develop transcendental knowledge of self if we remain "blissfully unaware" of our personal guna and karma? It is hardly possible to transcend it until you know what it is that you must first transcend. The planets are lords of our destiny in the fields of the signs, and they symbolically indicate the level of our cultural as well as metaphysical development. They also indicate our weaknesses and susceptibilities. Self knowledge entails knowing their influences; the worn cliché that the planets impel but do not compel is generally misunderstood. Whenever we are forced to do something, it can ultimately be traced to planetary influence (with rare exceptions).

With our inner eye of intuition open, with prajna fully operative, we would see situations in advance and take advantage of them or avoid them. The planets are secondary causalities, and their influences can be transcended when we are linked with the primal causes governing universal affairs. This is eminently doable, although it sounds improbable at first.

We must transcend the egoistic desires issuing from the planets, because such desires are but a subtle form of conditioning. Sidereal knowledge can help in the evolution of this detachment. The planets are indeed an integral part of Jung's designated archetypes. They can entrap us, or they can be dovetailed to serve the cause of our expansion of consciousness and development of psychic power. The horoscope can be turned into something more than a mere symbolic tool. The demigods (archetypes) of the seven major planets represent cosmic intelligence. Like ourselves, they too are also servants. Sidereal astrology is supposed to get us in touch with the Kala Purusha, and, through Him, with the Cause of all causes. This should become *our* most important cause.

Real astrology is a combination of intellectual and intuitive currents, which combine in a splendid way. Any genuine occultist can learn or take advantage of the language and meaning of the symbols (sometimes subliminally), and proceed deeper into his or her own realization. Neither the planets nor their influences are mythological; psychological thinking reveals just how the whole operation is working. Intelligence in applying the principles of sidereal astrology is wanted. Otherwise, very conflicting results will eventually produce both doubt and faithlessness, culminating in total abandonment of the effort.

At the highest level, these planetary archetypes help us to develop our achintya-shakti or inconceivable powers. They help us tap some great potentials and faculties that lie dormant within. They help us to develop prowess. This facilitation can only be had via a combination of yoga along with genuine astrological knowledge. It is a mystic process of reintegration and rejuvenation. It can produce the realization of impersonal truth—what was called the "white light" back in the Sixties.

Only a few astrologers or students of astrology reach this level, and certainly no one at the beginning stages of the process can achieve it. You have to be a transcendentalist—and a somewhat advanced one at that—in order to actuate such a realization. Although the study here is elevated, it is nevertheless universal. i.e., astrological knowledge is not, and can never be, transcendental knowledge. It can, however, be dovetailed in such a way that it supplements spiritual advancement.

At a level just below the aforementioned, the archetypes of the planets serve to represent myriad higher principles, such as ideals found in art, cinema, religion, philosophy, and (sometimes) in science. The astrologers or students at this level are mostly in the mode of goodness. These influences are what Ouspensky referred to as "B" influences, and there is some transformational value to be found in them. Here, the mind is controlled by intelligence, and the astrological symbolism serves to awaken intuition. The process needs to be rooted in spiritual culture. This stage is mostly beyond selfishness and the labyrinth of lower passions.

The astrological stage below this one brings us fully into the "A" influences. The astrologer progressively realizes that the planets govern and influence all human affairs ceaselessly. The students here are mostly in the mode of passion. At this stage, the planets are also seen as archetypes, their cosmic energies more or less toying with human beings in various ways. At this level, some separation enters the mix: These demigods (planets) are dovetailed to fulfill human desires, although they are still recognized and respected as the controllers and facilitators of results. There is a lack of complete awareness as compared to the higher stage.

Corruption enters at the lowest stage of astrological study. The process here degenerates entirely to the physical and lower astral plane. The planets are exploited by the astrologer. Conversely, they eventually gain complete control over the man or woman who enters into a kind of mundane pact or symbiosis with them. They then cover the higher intelligence of the person contaminated in this way and entangle him or her more and more in false ego. All "B" influences here either go unrecognized or are simply degraded into "A" influences, which only have temporary value. Persons at this stage find no ultimate meaning to their lives.

People who utilize astrology at this level are after fulfillment in the form of external objects for sense gratification. The ignorant mode predominates. Ultimately, this astrologer is victimized by the various planets he initially exploits. He eventually becomes possessed by some of them. These kinds of people are more often than not involved in black magic. The planets for them are actuated on a lower octave. It is no wonder that the planets are often considered demons by these kinds of occultists.

Anyone who takes to astrology with too much false ego, too little respect, too many misunderstandings, and too many material desires is a prime candidate for eventually coming under total control of the Law of Accident. We should not go there; witchcraft is risky business. Sidereal astrology is occult study, but not all occultists are witches.

Taking mastery over the planets entails transcending exploitation. The planets are actually meant to help awaken us from our slumber in illusions and delusions. One of the reasons that astrology has become twisted—to the point that genuine sidereal astrology is hardly even recognized in Western cultures—is that so many practitioners come to it from this lowest level. It is then prone to produce distortion. Somewhat ironically, it is the planets themselves which make sure that it does.

The need to present a new paradigm for astrology—one that eventually becomes widespread in the West—has never been more urgent nor more possible than it is now. The international technologies of communication today are really quite astounding. Nevertheless, what appears to be an imminent social breakdown jeopardizes all of this. Sidereal astrology is useful in all fields of life, particularly in its form of election astrology. The signs or constellations represent the field of activity in which the planets act; they spell out the limitation or possibilities. They are not meant to act as networks of entanglement; they are meant to display how we can structure our lives in terms of function.

The planets at their lower octaves represent features of a conditioned self that is struggling for existence within various fields of resistance and limitation. At the higher octave, when we add yoga, the sidereal science dovetails to a transcendental aim. We should not limit our intelligence to memory alone; there are new realizations we can gain, and sidereal astrology can help us to gain them. It is ultimately a dynamic tool, guided by powerful archetypes that constantly interact with us. This interaction is meant for transformation of consciousness from absorption in matter.

The astral rays can eventually all become at least indirectly helpful to our entering a calm, peaceful state of meditation. The planets, one way or another, represent our guna and karma. Once we become advanced in this science, much of that can be dovetailed to the cause of the Kala Purusha. If we do not take this human opportunity to integrate the energies of the planets into our creative intelligence, disillusionment with the Absolute principles and teachings will inevitably set in.

This book leads you past any and all superficialities that trend in that direction. It uplifts you from the whirlpool of disintegration toward integration. It acts as a springboard for further enlightenment, culminating in preliminary rejuvenation. Ignorance is our great enemy, and Truth is our great friend. This is your opportunity to take advantage of sidereal astrology. An advanced primer is herein being presented in a clear and concentrated way for what might be the very first time.

Chapter One

METHOD AND SCALE

There are sacred Vedic texts from India that describe, in voluminous and meticulous detail, the sidereal science of astrology. You would have to have a tremendous memory in order to even keep within your intelligence a section of these texts. Originally, the system was called Jyotish, but most of these texts do not include any such Sanskrit term in their titles. I do not attempt to impress you by including an extensive bibliography in this book; as a matter of fact, I don't include one at all. Instead, in this chapter, I tell you of my sources and method.

As far as the aforementioned sacred texts are concerned, I concentrate on only two of them. Those two are the Brihaj-jataka by Varahamihira and the Brihat Parashara Hora by Parashara. I have (what I hope is) the BJ in its original Sanskrit with an erudite commentary, and this book has a transliteration (word-by-word) breakdown of the verses. As such, I give it priority. Also, despite the fact that I am indebted to Swami Vijnanananda for his commentary, I have found some errors in a few of its transliterations and translations. Nevertheless, the book is a treasure house of sidereal knowledge and wisdom.

I do not have the Sanskrit for the partial translation of the BPH that I have secured. That's a setback obviously, but I am able to figure out the discrepancies—when I find them—by application of logic and intelligence via a comparative analysis with the Brihaj-jataka. The translation of the BPH has an arcane Hindu flavor to it (unlike the BJ commentary), and that's another reason why I give it secondary status to the translation by Vijnanananda Swami of Belur Math.

Aside from these direct Sanskrit or sacred texts on the science, I also have access to a sophisticated software program, which is helpful. It provides various interpretations based on a cornucopia of Vedic texts on the subject, but I take any or all of them with a big grain of salt.

There is also the book entitled Muhurtha by the late B.V. Raman, a renowned sidereal astrologer in South India. The knowledge in that book has been accessed for this one, particularly in the chapter that delineates election astrology, of course.

There is also a book written in the Eighties compiled by an American astrologer. It has some vitiated suppositions in it—the part that I find the most appalling is a horoscope supposedly of my spiritual master. This chart is flat-out wrong in two important areas: It contains a wrong lagna (ascendant) and it puts the Moon in the wrong sign. This will be discussed more fully as a small part of the instructional course; that course is meant to bring you to the third level of understanding in this science. Nevertheless, that book by the American astrologer, written entirely in English and fairly well-organized, has been helpful to me, and I mostly appreciate it.

There is also another book by a Western author on this topic that has provided some useful and general reference material. Since I do not quote any of these books directly, and since I do not plagiarize them, I do not consider it mandatory to list them. Another reason I do not list them is that such a step is an indirect form of advertising. I do not wish to advertise them, because they are flawed. I have been able to find the gold nuggets when consulting them, and you get to take advantage of that.

My method constitutes a presentation based upon sacred Vedic texts, direct commentary of such verses, and corollary books written on or about the science. However, for the purposes of clarity and effective impression, I also employ logic. Sometimes logic is called *eliminatio logica* in Latin, meaning that, when it is air-tight, it eliminates everything that is contradictory to it. I like that kind of logic, but I always recognize that the sacred texts are superior to it. That does not mean that logic should not be used; indeed, the science is called astro-*logical*.

Finally, and as a subsidiary contribution, my method also employs philosophical speculation. There is a gulf of difference between such speculative philosophy and mental speculation; they are as different as platinum and iron. Mental speculation tries to figure out "truths" that contradict and oppose Vedic conclusions, as well opposition to the essence of the Vedic conclusions, the Vaishnava siddhantas. I never engage in it.

Philosophical speculation, on the other hand, tries to figure out or realize truths that are not directly accessible via Vedic translations or speculates on knowledge that may have never been written down in the first place. Speculative knowledge is part of the comprehensive yoga system described in the Vedic literature, and praised (to some extent) even in the <u>Bhagavad gita</u> (<u>Geetopanishad</u>), which is the topmost Upanishad.

According to <u>Bhagavad-gita</u>, one should make research, by philosophical speculation, into the nature of spirit soul; one should make research in order to understand the spirit self. In the beginning, astrological research can be a key component of that search. I talk about this in other places in my book. It is an indirect process, granted. Nevertheless, such analysis can be helpful—as long as it does not directly contradict sacred text.

In Sanskrit, this process is called tattva-jnanartha-darshanam. This means that the knowledge (jnana) of reality or truth (tattva) can be gained (artha) through the process of philosophical speculation (darshanam). The Sanskrit word darshanam generally means direct realization (vijnanartham), but, in this verse from the Thirteenth chapter of <u>Bhagavad gita</u>, it refers to philosophical speculation. This is analysis used, progressively and spiritually, in the right direction.

Intelligence directly employed in the interest and service of the Absolute Truth, Who is the Supreme Person in the ultimate issue, is the highest use of intelligence (buddhi-yoga). That process is indirectly what this book is about; a kind of sankhya-yoga is used here. The process of philosophical speculation—by which, very gradually, one may come to the point of self-realization in buddhi-yoga—is a tertiary component of this book.

Now, let us proceed to scale. By scale, I am of course referring to different levels. This book is written in order to bring you to the second level of understanding in relation to the sidereal science. That is why I call it an advanced primer. In my instructional course (consult Appendix One), I shall offer to teach you the third level, if you are interested. However, if your magnetic center has now directed you to this book, then you now have facility to upgrade from level one to level two. I prefer to use the more precise term *octave* when referring to any of these levels.

An octave also denotes a process. There is a process in the matter of assimilating what I am presenting here. Octave one of this science would include all of tropical astrology and the basics or first principles of the sidereal science. As I am not fond of tropical astrology (although, now and then, I find something useful and revealing in it), I do not present any of its principles of interpretation in this primer. I do present the first principles of the sidereal science, however. If and/or when you choose to upgrade to octave three, I have provided a way for you to do so. Astrological realization usually proceeds according to scale.

One last note: Should any astute occultists or transcendentalists find some direct Vedic text that contradicts any part of this book (a part that involves philosophical speculation), feel free to contact me. I shall keep a list of all my customers and how I originally contacted them, including even addresses and phone numbers in some cases. If I become convinced that you have nailed it, I'll acquiesce to the higher presentation. Sacred text must always prevail (satyam eva jayate). In such a case, I'll contact each and every one of my students with the new information or revelation.

Chapter Two

AYANAMSHA

The tropical year is the duration it takes the Sun to travel from one vernal equinox to the next vernal equinox, and it is approximately three hundred sixty-five and a quarter days in length. The sidereal year is the duration of time it takes for the Sun to travel from and back to any fixed point in the stellar zodiac (in relation to a star in the fixed or immovable zodiac), and it is approximately 365.25 days in duration. The duration of the tropical year and the sidereal year are very similar—but they are not identical. Because they are not *exactly* of the same duration of time, the precession of the equinoxes has come into existence.

Currently—and you may be surprised why I employ this adverb (but that will be explained later)—the sidereal year is slightly longer than the tropical year. We can measure this very minute difference in terms of the sidereal arc that is traversed by the Sun during that differential between the two years. That difference now amounts to approximately fifty-four seconds of sidereal arc, or just short of one minute of sidereal arc. Sixty minutes equals one sidereal degree of arc, of course.

This difference adds up each year, increasing the overall or total precession of the equinoxes. It is a complex topic, but we have to understand it; we have to tackle it, in order to ascertain one important piece of information: **The ayanamsha**.

Now, the point in the zodiac where the vernal equinox begins each year, according to some astronomical historians, matched the very beginning of Aries back in antiquity, circa 400 A.D. The difference between the lengths of the tropical and sidereal years—being so very small—these two years back then were considered identical; the difference was not noticeable. Like compound interest, however, a small amount eventually amounts to something tangible. At this time, the precession is apparent.

The precession of the equinoxes has added up to such an extent that, when the vernal equinox begins in the third week of March each year, the Sun is still in the first third of *sidereal* Pisces—well over twenty degrees from the beginning of sidereal Aries.

Western astrologers are also known as tropical astrologers. They practice a system that assigns the first point of Aries in relation to the tropical year. Western astrology claims that the Sun enters Aries, its sign of exaltation, during the third week of March every calendar year. This we dispute. Sidereal astrologers say that the tropical or calendar year of the Sun has nothing whatsoever to do with the location of any planet situated in the zodiac. Sidereal or Eastern astrologers maintain that the signs are cent-per-cent determined by the fixed zodiac of stars.

Siderealists in the West (and many in the East, for that matter) also often use an emphemeris and a Tables of Houses to initially calculate the tropical placements of the planets. From these initial calculations, they deduct the ayanamsha. Indeed, the internal programming of virtually all (if not all) the sidereal software programs available to the English-speaking world has an ayanamsha inserted into the database.

In this chapter, I am presenting the standard understanding, the simplified explanation, of the ayanamsha. How planets function in the universal cosmography on the wheel of time is actually far more complex. For utilitarian purposes, there is no need to delve into that here. Especially in the last thirty years or so, an ayanamsha controversy has ensued amongst Western siderealists. You do not have to comprehend all of the complexities involved with it, but you should at least be aware of it. By having a general awareness, as presented in this chapter, you can take advantage of the knowledge of the precession of the equinoxes. An accurate ayanamsha is also provided at the end of this chapter.

In India, all planets were originally calculated according to somewhat complicated formulas contained in the Vedic siddhantas. The primary such siddhanta was (and still is) known as the Surya-siddhanta. This comprehensive treatise contains computations such as the ahargana, the cycles of the planets, their epicycles, and the ayanamsha calculation. The ayanamsha *in the Surya-siddhanta* is not used to determine the sidereal positions of the planets; it is employed in the calculation of lagna. Almost no one uses it only for that purpose at this time, however.

The ahargana and a planet's major cycle determines the mean position of a planet. The ahargana, or total sum of days (since the beginning of the current negative age to any given date at this time), combined with the general or major cycle of the planet, places that

24

planet somewhere in the zodiac. However, that's not where the planet really is or, in other words, that is not its true position. The planet's epicycle has to be employed in order to adjust its mean location to its true position.

Commentators on the Surya-siddhanta do not agree about the exact dimensions of these epicycles; there is a controversy in this area. The very great personality who perfectly delineated the epicycles (in his commentary on the Surya-siddhanta) was known as Bimal Prasad Datta. After his commentary was published and recognized by the learned men of his era, he then became known as Siddhanta Sarasvati. He was also the greatest spiritual master on Earth during the first half of the Twentieth Century, up to 1937 when he departed external manifestation.

The majority of Western astrologers who practice and employ sidereal astrology do not—and could not for that matter—comprehend the formulas of the Surya-siddhanta. Neither would most of them understand the complications of the epicycles nor would they know of the true epicycles given by Siddhanta Sarasvati. His epicycles are different from the "standard" epicycles accepted by most Hindu astrologers. Many of the astrologers of India still calculate planetary positions without using an ayanamsha, because they utilize formulas (including epicycles) contained in the siddhanta of their choice.

In the early Eighties, I checked into Western formulas used by American astronomers, i.e., how they calculated the positions of the planets in the tropical zodiac. I did this at a major collegiate center on the East Coast, very near Washington, D.C. I discovered that they utilize Neugenbauer's formulas. In analyzing his formulas, I was shocked to discover that they were mathematical calculations almost identical to those revealed in Surya-siddhanta. In fact, the only difference I could find between the two systems was a variation based upon Western parallax.

I personally consider it an impractical presupposition that planets can be perfectly and accurately placed in the zodiac via empiric measurements. By definition, these placements are made by fallible human empiricists taking advantage of man-made instruments in observatories. Have you ever really thought about this? Let me present you a comparative analysis.

Suppose we take a large marble and, somehow or other, suspend it up in the air, say fifty feet up, on a clear and full moon night.

A man is on his porch. Now, let the marble be about forty yards away, so that a telescope can (barely) pick it up. Beforehand, we have placed about twenty-five flashlights about one hundred and fifty yards beyond this marble, but those are only about, on average, thirty-five feet from ground level.

These flashlights are all pointed toward the man (with a tele-scope), and they are all turned on. They are arranged in a variegated pattern: Some are close, some are a little apart, some are higher, some are lower, some diagonal. The marble represents a planet, of course. The flashlights cumulatively represent the constellations in the back-ground. The band that they analogously represent is approximately seven degrees of zodiacal arc.

Now, with the marble suspended slightly above and before this band (also many yards away from the man with the telescope on his porch), how can he *accurately* determine the relation between the marble and the flashlights? He cannot. The reason is that there are so many variables. He can make a *reasonably* accurate *approximation*. However, that could be off by the equivalent of one degree or more of zodiacal arc.

The point here is that planetary positions were not and are not determined by empiric efforts in observatories; they are determined by *formulas*. Math *formulas* are used to compile an ephemeris, not empirical judgments. Those mathematically-calculated positions will accord with empiric evidence to a significant degree. In other words, one empiricist at a given observatory will swear by his formula, based upon his observations. Another empiricist will place the planet *in the same vicinity* as his competitor. However, he will not place it at the same exact degree, minute, and second of sidereal arc as his peer. This will be the case, of course, because his formula differs.

This discussion appears tangential, but it is relevant to the aya-namsha. The ayanamsha controversy cannot be resolved by telescopic or empirical observation. The ayanamsha is nothing more (or less) than a *shortcut* for determining the final, actual, or true position of any planet. It is also used now to determine the point of lagna, but in a different way than it was used in the ancient siddhantas. In using the ayanamsha, the Western ephemeris and Tables of Houses provide the basis. Whatever ayanamsha is used, it cannot provide perfect re-sults; this is because it is only an *approximation*. There is no one per-fect ayanamsha.

There cannot ever be one. Here's the secret that few know and even fewer share: The positions of the planets (via Western formulas) all individually have an inbuilt variance, i.e., a small anomaly. The formulas used today all have small imperfections, but just not the same imperfections in relation to each planet. These variances are minute, of course. In order to have any planet determined exactly, only the formulas of the <u>Surya-siddhanta</u>, combined with accurate epicycles, will produce such a resultant.

In other words, in order to use the ayanamsha method with complete accuracy, *slightly differing ayanamshas* would have to be deducted from each of the planets separately; each planet would have its own ayanamsha. No sidereal astrologer is going to do that, and no sidereal programmer is going to consider it, either. It would be a non-starter. Besides, these separate ayanamshas could only be ascertained if one was a master of the <u>Surya-siddhanta</u> formulas. If one was an adept in that astronomical discipline, why would he even bother deducting planetary ayanamshas? He would have no need for any such shortcut.

You should understand now that the ayanamsha controversy is rooted in calculations far more complicated than some astrologers realize. It appears to be a superficial controversy, but only at first glance. The great B.V. Raman summed it up well when he called it "a kind of hell." We concur completely. Every sidereal astrologer will swear by his or her ayanamsha. Most of them accept the Lahiri ayanamsha; after that, Raman's is the most used throughout India and the rest of the world.

However, the ayanamsha is integral, because you must place your planet where it actually is—or very, very close to where it actually is—in order to take advantage of the sidereal science. You need each planet in its correct sign, its correct navamsha, and its correct dvadasamsha. This requires an accurate ayanamsha. And if you place it in wrong subdivisions? Well, the shad-vargas are used to determine the sthana-bala or positional strength of each of the seven major planets. When calculation of the vargas (dreshkana, navamsha, dvadasamsha, trimsamsha) come up with conflicting locations—due to differing ayanamshas—you get different interpretations of results. That is simply not acceptable. The location of your planet computes differently according to different ayanamshas.

Of course, in actuality, it does not. The location of each planet stays right where it was at the time of your first breath. What does change is your placement, analysis, and interpretation of it. Using one wrong ayanamsha, and then analyzing your chart via another inaccurate ayanamsha, is no more valuable that jumping from one illusion to an entirely different one.

Originally, as mentioned in the Preface, I utilized the Lahiri ayanamsha. Later, I switched over to Raman's. In part, I made the switch because Raman cited K.N. Dutta of Bengal as the source of his ayanamsha. Raman was probably referring to Kedarnath Datta, the father of the aforementioned Siddhanta Sarasvati. K.N. Datta was the previous name for a great spiritual master, later known throughout India as Bhaktivinode Thakur; he lived just a few years into the Twentieth Century.

I got better results with the Raman ayanamsha but eventually also found it wanting. So I continued to fine-tune my ayanamsha. Raman's is significantly shorter than Lahiri's, and I kept moving in that direction. Swami Vijnanananda, in his commentary to the Brihaj-jataka, indicated that the ayanamsha was in the neighborhood of twenty degrees at the time of his commentary. I came to my conclusive ayanamsha—and I am going to be presenting it to you at the end of this chapter—for the abovementioned reason in combination with two other important reasons.

I knew that my spiritual master's Moon was in Gemini, as he directly revealed that fact in one of his letters. All the popular ayanamshas place it at the end of Taurus. Secondly, I had been studying my own chart since 1978. Having entered the second half of the cruise, I knew in detail what had gone on in my life. So I considered the occupational navamshas that three planets (determining it) would be in as per different ayanamshas. I did this especially in light of my avocational efforts throughout all my previous years; I shall be discussing this topic of occupation later in this book. My occupational engagements could only make sense if the three planets which determined them where in specific navamshas. That was the ultimate verification I required to make the decision.

Could my ayanamsha be off by some minutes of sidereal arc? Of course it could. Indeed, as aforementioned, to place every planet perfectly, each planet would require its own ayanamsha. The comparative discrepancies or minor adjustments between and amongst them would be very small, so this factor should not be blown out of proportion. You don't have to have a *perfect* ayanamsha. What you need is an *accurate* ayanamsha, especially for proper navamsha and dvadasamsha placement. The ayanamsha I am giving you will produce those results, because it has been triple-checked for accuracy, as abovementioned.

If you want absolute perfection, let me only encourage you in that exalted desire. Study the Surya-siddhanta under an astronomical guru and utilize the epicycles of Srila Bhaktisiddhanta Sarasvati Gosvami Prabhupada, as previously mentioned. Then, if you turn the corner, you will know *exactly* where each of your planets was situated at the time of your birth. If you want to take a shortcut like 99.9% of every other sidereal astrologer on earth, then use the ayanamsha I am giving you.

There is no Age of Aquarius; never has been one and never will be one. The ayanamsha never goes into Aquarius, because it is a libration. You can picture it as a pendulum. The ayanamsha swings between three degrees Pisces and twenty-seven degrees Aries, as per Surya-siddhanta. It is slowing at this time. When it reaches its abovementioned boundary in Pisces, the tropical year and the sidereal year will be of equal duration. After that, exactly opposite to the case now, the tropical year will gradually become longer than the sidereal year.

Since the current rate of change for the precession of the equinoxes is approximately fifty-four seconds of sidereal arc per year (or nine-tenths of one minute of sidereal arc per year), the same ayanamsha is repeated in the table once every ten years. For the sake of convenience, I did not employ seconds of sidereal arc but simply rounded the ayanamsha to the nearest minute of sidereal arc. You read the table in this way: 21-36 is an ayanamsha of twenty-one degrees and thirty-six minutes. The correlations are straightforward.

1950	21-16
1951	21-17
1952	21-18
1953	21-19
1954	21-20
1955	21-21
1956	21-22
1957	21-23
1958	21-24
1959	21-24
1960	21-25
1961	21-26

1962	21-27
1963	21-28
1964	21-29
1965	21-30
1966	21-31
1967	21-32
1968	21-33
1969	21-33
1970	21-34
1971	21-35
1972	21-36
1973	21-37
1974	21-38
1975	21-39
1976	21-40
1977	21-41
1978	21-42
1979	21-42
1980	21-43
1981	21-44
1982	21-45
1983	21-46
1984	21-47
1985	21-48
1986	21-49
1987	21-50
1988	21-51
1989	21-51
1990	21-52
1991	21-53
1992	21-54
1993	21-55
1994	21-56
1995	21-57
1996	21-58
1997	21-59
1998	22-00
1999	22-00
2000	22-01
2001	22-02

2002	22-03
2003	22-04
2004	22-05
2005	22-06
2006	22-07
2007	22-08
2008	22-09
2009	22-09
2010	22-10
2011	22-11
2012	22-12
2013	22-13
2014	22-14
2015	22-15
2016	22-16
2017	22-17
2018	22-18
2019	22-18
2020	22-19
2021	22-20

Chapter Three

BENEFICS AND MALEFICS

The Western version of astrology has a misunderstanding about benefics and malefics. To cite just one example, they generically consider the Sun to be benefic and the Moon to be malefic. Accurately determining benefics and malefics is the most important feature for understanding your horoscope. However, it is complicated: The understanding proceeds via three levels, and we shall refer to them as octaves.

The first level, the first octave, constitutes the basic rules. These rules delineate the *fundamental* benefics and malefics. The Brihaj-jataka and the Brihat Parashara Hora are in agreement concerning this first octave.

Here are those basic rules: Saturn is intrinsically a great malefic and only becomes a benefic when exalted, in its own signs, or the yogakaraka of the chart. Mars is your garden-variety malefic; he becomes a benefic when exalted or in his own signs, and also as yogakaraka. Sun is called krura; he is mischievous and a malefic, generically—but he is not as malefic as Mars. Sun is a benefic when exalted, in his own sign, or yogakaraka.

A yogakaraka is a planet that owns both a quadrant and a trine. The Sun and the Moon only own one sign; they are never yogakarakas. Mercury and Jupiter are also never yogakarakas, but that is for a different reason. Mars is the yogakaraka for Cancer and Leo ascendants. Saturn is the yogakaraka for Venus ascendants (Taurus and Libra); Venus for Saturn ascendants.

Mercury is generically benefic when he is alone in a sign, except in debilitation. When conjunct a malefic, he becomes malefic; this is only his first status, however. When conjunct both a benefic and a malefic, he will take on the quality of the closest conjunct planet; if they are more or less of equal proximity, then he will remain a benefic. When Mercury is conjunct the Sun and not combust, he forms budha-aditya yoga; he cannot be a malefic in that configuration. The Moon is a benefic when waxing and a malefic when waning. However, when the Moon is combust, even if waxing, he is a malefic (a weak one). All planets are weak malefics when combusted by the Sun. Venus is a benefic except when combust or debilitated; this same rule applies to Jupiter, the most benefic planet.

An exalted planet is always a benefic, despite whatever house(s) it has in its lordship portfolio. Any and all combust planets are automatically malefics with little power; the silver lining here is that they really can do little or no damage to the house they tenet.

According to the rules of neecha-bhanga raja-yoga, the malefic status produced by debilitated planets is lifted under certain circumstances. Some opine that this makes them great benefics; my experience has taught me otherwise. It more or less merely lifts the intensity of their malignant qualities, except when they are also combust.

According to the rules of neecha-bhanga raja-yoga, the malefic status produced by a debilitated planet is lifted, and here are the rules:

1) The debilitated planet is in a quadrant from Sun, Moon, or from lagna, and this does include a debilitated planet in the ascendant;

2) The debilitated planet is in a quadrant from a planet that would be exalted in the sign in which the debilitated planet is situated;

3) The debilitated planet is in a sign wherein the planet, which would be exalted in that sign, is itself in a quadrant from lagna, the Sun, or the Moon;

4) The debilitated planet is exalted in navamsha.

Combustion of the planets is as follows: Moon within 12 degrees of the Sun; Mars within 17; Mercury within 14; Jupiter within 11; Venus within 10; Saturn within 15. If Mercury is retrograde, then the margin is 12; if Venus is retrograde, then his margin for combustion is only eight degrees.

Let us now proceed to the next level of this determination. That involves the application of the basics in terms of those being *only the preliminary principles*—which then become changed for many of the planets in your chart. Knowing which of the planets are initially benefics, and which are initially malefics, is required; this is especially the case in relation to planetary lordships of quadrants four, seven, and ten.

The basic rules at this level are these: The lord of the lagna is a benefic or a favorable neutral planet. The lord of a quadrant and a trine is better than a benefic; he is the yogakaraka of the chart, i.e., the most prominent planet in it. The lords of the third, the sixth, the eighth, the eleventh, and the twelfth are usually malefic, unless they are a fundamental benefic and also the lord of a trine. The lord of the second house is a killer but neutral. Benefics generally become malefics if they are lords of quadrants—even if they own two quadrants, as is the case with Jupiter for a Gemini ascendant. The lords (or lord) of the seventh and second houses are marakas (planets that kill).

This book is a primer on the subject of sidereal astrology. Octave three for determining benefics and malefics is delineated in C.O.R.E. Sidereal Astrology, my instructional manual for those occultists who wish to become C.O.R.E. Astrologers (see Appendix One). That is what this book now in your hands facilitates, i.e., it helps a beginner make initial judgments of his astrological strengths and weaknesses, without getting lost in the labyrinth of interrelated details that are to be assimilated at higher levels.

Planets, even if they are malefics, still do good for their own signs when posited in or aspecting those houses. The planets can have their statuses altered, even after determining if they are benefics or malefics. One example of this would be when two benefics bracket a malefic in the same sign; that malefic is going to have some of his negative influence neutralized; of course, the bracketing benefics are affected adversely.

You must know whether a planet is a benefic or a malefic (in respect to the length of the dasha (life stage) of that planet) when he is in houses above the horizon. This will be explained in C.O.R.E. Sidereal Astrology. It is a very meticulous and exacting calculation which determines the length of the dashas and the length of life. If length of a dasha is calculated based on a planet initially being a malefic—when, in actuality, due to house lordship, it has been converted in a benefic—wrong conclusions result.

Sometimes, Mercury is considered by tropical astrologers to be a malefic when retrograde. Sidereal astrology has a different interpretation of retrograde planets, especially when they are ultimately found to be benefics. When Mercury or any other benefic is retrograde, its effect in a chart is to create idiosyncrasies or eccentricities in its portfolios. A retrograde planet attains full chestha-bala; he is, more often than not, strong. His being retrograde in a chart has no effect on Mercury's status. This is also the case for Venus. However, when malefic Mars or Saturn are retrograde, they then become more powerful malefics.

The planets also produce a person's misconceptions; how could it be otherwise? Obviously, the planets do not allow unqualified persons to understand astrology at higher levels; they do not want a person with the wrong attitude and improper eligibility to understand this confidential sidereal science—and they make sure that he or she does not.

This book is an advanced primer of sidereal astrology. It is important that you understand your benefics and malefics, and the preliminary knowledge explained here, in a concise, clear, and organized way, helps you do that. The final rules for determining benefics and malefics are statements in the sacred texts; some of them appear contradictory. However, a very careful analysis reveals the logic and applications behind the statements and rules in those sacred texts when the final determination of the planet (in terms of it being a benefic or malefic) is made.

These rules will be given in the instructional course; the preliminary principles are explained here. Varahamihira did not even go this far in his book, although there is always the possibility that he did do so (and that section was culled out over time). You are free to consult a translation of <u>Brihat Parashara Hora</u> in the meantime to see if you can understand it.

Chapter Four

PRIMARY PRINCIPLES

Sidereal astrology obviously must commence with first principles, although you will also be given some advanced primary knowledge as well in this treatise. Indeed, there are some metaphysical and astrological explanations that you will receive here that may have never before been revealed. So, for those of you who already know astrology to some degree, kindly bear with the delineation of the basic principles. After all, a complete beginner is not really at a disadvantage in this study, because he or she does not have to unlearn or re-learn anything.

There are seven major planets, two minor or shadow planets (known as Rahu and Ketu), and twelve signs in the zodiac. The signs always exactly correspond to the houses in sidereal astrology. The Sun and the Moon each rule one of these twelve signs; the other five major planets rule two.

The names of the signs are: Aries, Taurus, Gemini, Cancer, Leo, Virgo, Libra, Scorpio, Sagittarius, Capricorn, Aquarius, and Pisces. In order, these signs are ruled by Mars, Venus, Mercury, Moon, Sun, Mercury, Venus, Mars, Jupiter, Saturn, Saturn, and Jupiter. A sign consists of thirty degrees of sidereal arc, and, obviously, the zodiac consists of three hundred and sixty degrees of sidereal arc.

Each sign is divided into two equal parts, one governed by the Sun and the other by the Moon. These particular subdivisions are called horas. The next major subdivision is called a dreshkana (decanate), and it consists of one-third of each sign, constituting ten degrees of sidereal arc. The most important subdivision comes next: Navamsha. It is one-ninth of a sign, consisting of three degrees and twenty minutes of sidereal arc. Next comes the dvadasamsha, which divides the sign into twelve equal parts of two degrees and thirty minutes each.

Finally comes the trimsamsha; each trimsamsha is one degree. So, technically, there are thirty of them per sign, but, in reality, it is a little different from that. Ascertaining the exact trimsamsha for any given planet in a horoscope is much easier than ascertaining its exact dvadasamsha portion. This is because the trimsamshas are grouped in amalgamated sets of degrees, which are each governed by one planet.

These then are your six pre-eminent divisions of any sign, in accordance with any specific planetary placement: Its rashi (sign), its hora, its dreshkana, its navamsha, its dvadasamsha, and its trimsamsha. Sometimes you will read about the shad-vargas of a planet; that term refers to these six subdivisions of a sign (of course, the sign itself is not a subdivision, but it is a one-twelfth subdivision of the total zodiac). In order to know the divisions and subdivisions of any one of your planetary placements, an accurate ayanamsha is essential; I have provided it previously.

There is yet another important subdivision of the zodiac. It applies differently in relation to the signs of the zodiac, because, unlike the shad-vargas, it overlaps many of the signs. This subdivision is called a nakshatra, and it consists of thirteen degrees and twenty minutes of sidereal arc. As far as the horoscope is concerned, there are twenty-seven such nakshatras or lunar mansions. However, there is another nakshatra known as abhijit that is not really much connected to the main part of the ecliptic like the other twenty-seven; it is distinctly north of the band on which all of the others are closely situated.

In my experience, the nakshatra placement of the Moon is a very important study, and Varahamihira indirectly confirms this in his <u>Brihaj-jataka</u>. He devotes more or less one whole chapter to the effects of the Moon being in each of the twenty-seven nakshatras, which are also known as constellations. In his book, there is no emphasis on how the other six major planets are affected by their placement in various nakshatras. As such, we shall also concentrate on the lunar placements in the constellations.

Returning to the signs themselves, they are also divided into different categories. Aries, Cancer, Libra, and Capricorn are known as moveable signs. Taurus, Leo, Scorpio, and Aquarius are fixed signs, and the other four signs are known as mixed signs. There is another classification as well: Aries, Leo, and Sagittarius are fire signs; Taurus, Virgo, and Capricorn are earth signs; Gemini, Libra, and Aquarius are air signs, and Cancer, Scorpio, and Pisces are known as water signs.

Tables will be provided at the end of the book in relation to the lords of the various vargas or subdivisions. There are some shortcuts to memorizing the order of the lords of these divisions, but I leave that up to you to figure out for yourself, if you are interested in doing so. The patterns are not at all difficult to discern.

The junctions between Cancer (a water sign) and Leo (a fire sign), as well as between Scorpio and Sagittarius and between Pisces and Aries are known as gandantharas. Technically, they are known as sign gandantharas. These junctions are inauspicious and can even be dangerous when the Moon, in particular, is transiting them. They will be described in more detail in the chapter on election astrology.

Aries, Taurus, Gemini, Cancer, Sagittarius, and Capricorn are night signs and are powerful during the night. The other six signs are day signs and are powerful during daytime. The signs are said to represent our desires, feelings, passions, emotions, and the whole of consciousness that is dependent upon experience. Planets and houses represent specific things, specific functions, etc.

It is also described that the odd-numbered signs (Aries, Gemini, Leo, etc.) are both male and malefic, while the even-numbered signs are female and benefic. This generality can be pretty much discarded, however, because any sign can either turn out to be very good or very bad for you, depending on different situations and numerous other factors. The odd signs are more connected to life functions and even signs to formatory considerations.

There are many such descriptions of the signs that may be a bit interesting but have little or no pragmatic value; I see no reason to delineate all of that. This book is condensed and concentrated knowledge; it is not designed for casual reading ventures. It will not attract that kind of customer. What I reveal and expound upon here are what, from my experience, are the primary or important facets of astrological knowledge. This includes features or qualities that are relevant to practical endeavors.

Now we come to the topic of planetary exaltations and debilitations. A table will also be provided in Appendix Two listing each planet, its sign of exaltation, and the degree in that sign where it is at peak exaltation. It is debilitated in the exact opposite sign, and its peak debilitation follows the same principle. The degrees of peak exaltation are not ultra-important; if you have a planet in its sign of exaltation, it is very good for you.

Then there are further considerations of strengths. One of these is called Mula Trikona, and table has been provided for it. It is interesting to notice that Mercury and Moon are exalted in the same signs in which they are further strengthened by Mula Trikona. In actuality, however, they are exalted in part of the sign and in mula trikona in the other part; in Mercury's case, in his own sign in another part.

There is also vargottama strength, relating to the navamsha position of a planet. If the planet's placement in both sign and navamsha are the same, he is vargottama. Planets are, of course, lords of the various navamshas, based upon the corresponding signs of the zodiac. For example, a planet may be in the sign of Aquarius and also found to be in a navamsha of Saturn. If that navamsha corresponds to Capricorn, vargottama is not attained. If it corresponds to Aquarius, however, then that is what is called vargottama.

Each sign of the zodiac, at the time of a birth or an initiative, corresponds to one of twelve divisions known as houses; the chart is divided into these twelve houses. This is called equal house division. I advise you not to accept the bhava-chalita calculation for house placement nor the other speculations that divide houses. Let me explain these to you.

The signs are of different lengths in the northern and southern hemispheres. Since the majority of my readers are in the northern hemisphere, I shall discuss it in terms of that sphere. Here, Capricorn, Aquarius, Pisces, Aries, Taurus, and Gemini are smaller signs than the other six; this situation exacerbates the farther north you proceed in longitude. As such, say you have a Gemini ascendant for a birth in London. London is quite far north, so the sign of Aries is not very big at that latitude. Say you have four planets in Aries, one just barely in Taurus, and one at the tail end of Pisces. Now, in the bhava-chalita, all six of those planets would be put into the eleventh. I am advising you not to form your charts or your calculations or your judgments in terms of this idea; I consider a concoction.

The other speculation is a bit easier to understand, but just as invalid (according to my perspective, of course). If your point of the ascendant is at or very near fifteen degrees, then this concoction would be a non-starter. However, as an example, say that your point of the ascendant (the point of that sign that was on the eastern horizon at the moment of birth) was five degrees of Scorpio. This other divided sign/house theory says that your first house has a midpoint of five degrees. As such, the first house is then thought to extend from twenty degrees of Libra to twenty degrees of Scorpio. If you had a planet at the tail of end of Scorpio, the theory postulates that this planet would actually be in the second house.

However, it is actually in the first. The signs correspond to the houses in classic sidereal astrology, and this is what I teach both in this primer (octave two) as well as in my instructional course (octave three).

Lagna point is important *in another way*, and this will be discussed in due course. However, if the ascendant (also known as lagna) happens to have its point of lagna at one degree or at twenty-nine degrees of a sign, it does not really matter. That sign will fully correspond with the ascendant, also known as the first house. As such, the next sign will fully correspond with the second house, the sign after that with the third house, etc. It may seem "logical" to speculate otherwise, but that is not the teaching of the classic sidereal system; it is another modern concoction.

Varahamihira condenses the nature of the twelve houses as follows: First house governs physical body; second, relatives; third, brothers and sisters; fourth, close friends; fifth, offspring; sixth, enemies; seventh, mate; eighth, death; ninth, good qualities and state of morality; tenth, profession, honor, and dignity; eleventh, casual or easy income; and twelfth, expenditure. Of course, all the elements and categories of life have their placements somewhere in one of these twelve houses. Varahamihira goes on to separately say this very same thing by describing that the first house also denotes determinative strength; the second, earned or accumulated wealth; third, bravery (or cowardice, its opposite, if afflicted); fourth, place of residence; fifth, sons (a repeat); sixth, wounds and injuries; seventh wife (another repeat); eighth, personal point of weakness; ninth, religion, father, and preceptor; tenth, honor and respectability (this is also the house of victory and success); eleventh, acquisition and gain; and twelfth, loss. As an additional note, the eleventh is also the house of social contacts and casual friends. The twelfth is also the house of incarceration and hospitalization.

Varahamihira goes on to term the tenth house as Ajna, which means command. This may be related in some way to the ajna chakra. We shall be describing the chakras (to a small degree) and the ordinary centers in more depth in another chapter, as per astrological synchronicity.

Speaking of the tenth, it is called a kendra (quadrant). The kendras are the prominent houses: The first, the fourth, the seventh, and the tenth. Then there are the trines. These are also important (but not prominent) and generally auspicious (unless afflicted). The first house (lagna), the fifth, and the ninth are the trines. The ascendant is both a kendra and a trine.

This fact should serve as a reminder of just how important the first house actually is. Lagna must be analyzed first when trying to understand any horoscope; the natal chart or janma-kundali pivots upon lagna. In election astrology, lagna is always given prime consideration.

The ascendant is analyzed in terms of the nature of the sign that corresponds to it, the dvadasamsha of the point of lagna (aforementioned, above), and the lord of lagna's placement in both sign and navamsha. Also, any planets in lagna obviously affect it either positively or negatively, as well as any planets in close conjunction to the lord of the ascendant. Although aspects on the lord of lagna are secondarily important, primary considerations have just been detailed. Aspects will be described in a later chapter.

The signs of the zodiac also have natures. These correspond to human, animal, reptile, or aquatic. Cancer and Scorpio are the reptile signs. Capricorn and Pisces are aquatic. Aries, Taurus, Leo, and Sagittarius are animal signs. Gemini, Virgo, Libra, and Aquarius are human signs. The reptile signs are significantly strengthened when they correspond to the seventh house. The aquatic signs are strengthened when corresponding to the fourth. The animals signs are strong corresponding to the tenth, and the human signs are strengthened when they are lagna.

In other words, these houses become significantly stronger when the aforementioned correspondences are operative. As you can see, houses are also to be judged in terms of strengths and weaknesses. For example, a Scorpio ascendant during a day birth would make the tenth potent, Leo being both a day sign and an animal sign. If a strong benefic was in the tenth—and its lord also strong and well-placed in the chart—the indications for great success, honor, and occupational placement would be high.

This chapter presents some basic principles in connection with signs. More fundamentals need to be explained in relation to the planets. As mentioned previously, all the technicalities involved in determining lagna via long-hand calculations will not be presented here. Simply secure a sound Vedic sidereal program with comprehensive features and tailor it according to the ayanamsha I have given you. Make sure to employ even house correspondences between the signs and houses. The planets will then be placed in their signs, houses, and subdivisions.

The Sun represents ego; this is called ahankara in Sanskrit. It is the false ego in the conditioned stage of material existence. The Moon represents the mind, especially the subconscious mind. Mars represents energy and vigor. Mercury represents speech and intelligence. Jupiter represents knowledge, happiness, and education. Venus represents passions and desires—some would say human love. Saturn represents pain and sorrow. The ascending node Rahu and the descending node Ketu are usually malefics. Rahu represents criminality, material enjoyment, and illusion. Ketu represents natural cataclysms and occult restrictions.

Now let us discuss the planets in terms of colors. By this is meant that every color in material existence, visible to our spectrum, has a specific planetary lord. I'm giving you something special here. There are common misunderstandings concerning the lords of the colors, but I shall clear them up for you now. Before proceeding, we must acknowledge that most of the planets will have more than one color in their portfolios. Astro-logically, which planet would have the most colors?

Color is based upon light. This comes to us from the Sun. As such, he should have numerous colors in his portfolio and such is the case. The Sun rules over red, brown, copper, and purple. All the distinct or bright hues of these colors are also ruled by the Sun. The very light pastels of these colors, however, are ruled by the Moon. Very dark versions of these colors are ruled by Saturn, as this planet rules black.

The Moon rules white, pink, and the pastels of all colors. Bright colors, however, are not under its rule; they stay with their own planet.

Mars rules orange. There are verifications. Fire is red to a child, but it is bright orange (not yellow or red; check it out sometime) after that stage. Restaurants secure revenue when they paint their walls orange, because it increases the fire in the belly, ruled by Mars.

Mercury rules green, including all combinations of this color such as forest green, turquoise, aqua dominated by green, etc.

Jupiter rules yellow and gold. Venus rules indigo and silver; there is also an indirect indication in BJ that multi-colors (such as opal) are ruled by Venus. Saturn rules blue, black, grey, and all smoky colors. He, as aforementioned, also rules very dark colors.

The Sun rules the eastern direction, Venus the southeast, Mars the south, Rahu the southwest, Saturn the west, Moon the northwest, Mercury the north, and Jupiter the northeast.

All planets are male controllers of universal affairs under the command of *Source* Universal. Obviously, the Moon and Venus have feminine energies in their portfolio. Planets are secondary causalities under the superintendence of the prime controllers, viz., Lord Vishnu, Lord Brahma, and Lord Shiva. The Cause of all causes is located in the spiritual world; Lord Vishnu is His direct representative here, as is *Source* Universal.

The planets represent general tendencies: In this context, the Sun, Jupiter, and Mars represent male tendencies; the Moon and Venus female ones. Mercury and Saturn represent hermaphroditic tendencies and personalities.

Jupiter and Venus are the lords of Aryan intellectuals. The Sun and Mars are the lords of warriors. The Moon is the lord of the mercantile or agricultural class of men. Mercury is the lord of workers. All of these classifications are in terms of the Aryan culture. It is Saturn, however, who rules the non-Aryans. Currently, most of the cultures of the world are non-Vedic or non-Aryan. Saturn rules their intelligentsia, warriors, businessmen, and employees, i.e., everybody in these degraded cultures.

There are three modes of material nature: Goodness, passion, and ignorance. Those in goodness are called sattvic personalities. Those in passion are called rajasic. Human beings in ignorance, who are only superficially different from the animals (or even lower) are called tamasic. Jupiter, the Moon, and the Sun represent the sattvic nature. Venus and Mercury represent the rajasic nature. Mars and Saturn represent the tamasic nature, and that's obviously a big part of the reason why these planets are so often malefics. Any culture implicated in animal slaughter, or any human being affiliated with that culture, is classified as tamasic. This book is meant to elevate you from that abominable status.

The predominant mode of an individual is his essential nature. There will be a separate chapter detailing this important discussion later on in the work. The Sun rules bones, the Moon rules blood, Mars rules bone marrow, Mercury rules skin, Jupiter rules fatty tissue, Venus rules semen, and Saturn rules nerves. The body of a person corresponds to the nature of the lord (or ruler) of the rising sign or the lord (or ruler) of the dvadashamsa of the point of lagna.

The Sun presides over places of worship, the Moon over wells and bodies of water, Mars over places for cooking and armaments, Mercury over places of entertainment, Jupiter over storerooms and treasuries, Venus over bedrooms, and Saturn over barren places. All other places have a corollary relationship with the one of those described here, and you can use your intelligence in order to discern which planet rules those other places. For example, the lavatory room would be ruled by Saturn.

The Sun has an affinity for the summer in general and is the lord of that season; he also is the lord of bright, sunny days. The Moon rules the monsoon season and rainy or heavily overcast days. Mars rules over unbearably hot days, conducive to forest fires. Mercury rules the mild, autumnal season. Jupiter rules days in which dew is prominent in the morning; this is called the hemanta season in India. Venus rules the spring. Saturn rules the winter, obviously.

The Sun rules coarse and thick cloth. The Moon rules brand new clothing. Mars rules cloth that is partially burnt. Mercury rules cloth that is still a bit wet. Jupiter rules cloth that is neither new nor old. Venus rules strongly-stitched cloth. Saturn rules torn and old clothing.

There are other divisions or systems of life in which the planets have their related portfolios of lordship; I have only mentioned the prominent ones here. In relation to this, an entire chapter of this book is devoted to the lordship of the *mundane* centers, those *corresponding to* the chakras.

There are six tastes; these are called rasas in Sanskrit. The Sun rules over hot and pungent tastes. The Moon rules over salty rasas (this makes sense, because the Moon also rules over the oceans, full of saltwater). Mars rules bitter tastes. Mercury rules over preparations where all the six rasas are represented. Jupiter rules over all that is sweet. Venus rules over all that is sour. Saturn rules over astringent foods, such as lettuce.

There is a formula presented by Varahamihinra for determining which planets are friends to some planets, neutral to others, and enemies of some other planets. First, you take the Mula Trikona place of any given planet. The planets that are rulers of the second from any given planet's Mula Trikona, the rulers of the fourth, from the fifth, from the eighth, from the ninth, and from the twelfth houses from that Mula Trikona place are the planet's friends. The other places are unfavorable. Also, the house that represents the place of exaltation for that planet is a friend, provided this planet does not also rule an unfavorable place. Obviously, if the Sun or Moon rules the second, etc. house from a planet's Mula Trikona sign, then it is a friend; otherwise, it is an enemy. When any other planet rules one of the six friendly places (including the house of exaltation of the planet being considered), but it also rules one of the six unfriendly houses, then that planet becomes a neutral or indifferent planet.

These are called the permanent relationships between and amongst the planets. When this is fine-tuned, in terms of the temporary relationships, the interrelationships in a given chart are ascertained. A Table in Appendix Two has been provided for clarification of these principles.

Looking at Mars, the Mula Trikona position of Mars is Aries. The second house ruler (of Taurus) is Venus, the fourth house from Aries is ruled by the Moon, the fifth house ruler is the Sun, the eighth house ruler is Mars himself, the ninth house ruler is Jupiter as is the twelfth house ruler. The Sun and the Moon, being the rulers of only one sign, are friends of Mars. Jupiter rules two houses, and both have been listed as friendly places. So, Jupiter is a friend to Mars.

Venus rules one favorable house and one unfavorable place, so Venus is neutral. Mercury rules two unfavorable houses, so Mercury is an enemy to Mars. Saturn apparently rules two unfavorable places, also. One of those is the place of exaltation for Mars. As such, Saturn is judged as an indifferent or neutral planet to Mars.

In Appendix Three, we shall delve into this subject even further. The importance of knowing the interrelationships of planets cannot be underestimated. In terms of benefics and malefics, a neutral (initial designation) planet can be turned into either a benefic or a malefic, due to the location of the lord of the sign he is in.

Chapter Five

GENERAL INTERPRETATION

Results are mostly to be predicted as per planetary positions. First, we need to consider interpretation of the Moon. In sidereal astrology, emphasis is given to the Moon, not to the Sun. *If the ruler of the navamsha where the Moon is situated is powerful, then you disregard the reading of the Moon in its sign.* Instead, you interpret the Moon as if it was situated in the sign of that powerful navamsha lord; the correspondences of the navamsha lords are found in Appendix Two. If the ruler of the Moon's navamsha is mediocre or weak, then interpret the Moon according to his sign placement.

When interpreting or judging a planet, you will find that his placement in a sign gets one reading and his placement in a house usually gets a somewhat different reading. There is a secret concerning this, in terms of how to use sidereal astrology for self-help and personal improvement. You conclude the nature and interpretation of a planet in terms of the connection he has to a sign and its subdivisions. The nature and interpretation of a house is determined by the planet or planets situated in that house, its vacancy (when that is the case), and its lord's placement.

There are three components in determining just how a planet will function in a given sign and house: 1) The strength of the sign, 2) the strength of the house, and 3) the strength of the lord of that sign. Obviously, this applies to the Moon and the other six major planets, as well.

If all three of these are strong, you will get the full effects described for that planet. If two of the three are strong, you will get two-thirds of the described effects. If only one of these three components is strong, you will only experience one-third of the described effects. The effects are virtually not present only if all three of these are weak. I am now going to present a concise reading or description of the Moon in the signs:

MOON IN ARIES: Mixed; lord is a friend. Modest eater, inclined to vegetarianism, acquiesces, loves outdoors, wanderer, generally lusty, unsteady income, heroic, sexually attractive, has an excellent service attitude; there will be facial and/or head wounds, afraid of water.

MOON IN TAURUS: Very good; lunar exaltation position. Handsome, attractive gait, face and sides get marked, unselfish, generous, power of endurance, ability to command, raised neck, phlegmatic, easily separated from friends, difficulty in saving money, fortunate, forgiving, strong sensual desires, attractive to opposite sex, a reliable friend, middle and later years are the most happy ones.

MOON IN GEMINI: Mixed; lord is a friend. Inclined toward sex and clever at obtaining it, intelligent, quick-witted, practical joker, tendency toward gambling, smooth talker, big eater, heavy into music, looks to create friendships with the timid.

MOON IN CANCER: Good; own sign. Influenced strongly by opposite sex, dedicated to friends and loves them, astrologically inclined, usually possesses houses, many noticeable ups and downs in life, moved by sweet words, likes gardening and the environment.

MOON IN LEO: Mixed; lord is a friend. Unselfish, charitable, dignified, calmly intelligent, great prowess, steady, respectful to mother, tendency toward anger, hates opposite sex, fond of meat-eating, nurses grudges, sometimes gets into trouble.

MOON IN VIRGO: Good; lord is a friend. Shy, generally happy, gentle, truthful, clever, expert in fine arts, versed in scripture, studies religion, possesses mental prowess, strongly sexual, exploits resources of others, a very sweet talker.

MOON IN LIBRA: Mixed; lord is neutral. Controlled by opposite sex, weak limbs, traveler, wealthy, tendency toward illnesses or afflictions, not covetous, usually wise, theistic, clever in trade, does good for his (or her) friends and relatives but gets criticized by them—and they leave him.

MOON IN SCORPIO: Very bad; place of debilitation. Afflicted by illness, loses role models early in life, dishonest, vile, secretive, likes privacy, favored by powerful people.

MOON IN SAGITTARIUS: Good; lord is a friend. Receives paternal inheritance, unselfish, charitable, can become an accomplished author.

MOON IN CAPRICORN: Mixed; lord is neutral. Loves family, graceful, listens to advice, good memory, fortunate, strong, composer, hypocritical in religion, traveler, covetous, illicit connections, ruthless, shameless.

MOON IN AQUARIUS: Bad; lord is neutral. Tendency toward varicose veins, hairy, rough, not very literate, engages in illicit connections with married people, vicious, many ups and downs in life, attracted to flowers, attached to friends, able to endure troubles.

MOON IN PISCES: Good; lord is a friend. Earns money through sales, enjoys the earnings of others, attached to his or her own property, affectionate to spouse, overcomes others but dominated by spouse, obtains wealth accidentally, beautiful eyes and body, learned.

Any debilitated planet is unwanted and indicates bad karma. However, as aforementioned in a previous chapter, the debilitation is mitigated by neecha-bhanga raja-yoga. Removing the debilitation in this way does not, from my experience, make that planet great, however. In other words, don't make too much of the Sanskrit word here, viz., raja-yoga. Neecha-bhanga simply makes a debilitated planet significantly improved.

We have looked at the Moon in his signs, so now let us check out how he fares in the twelve houses. The house placements for the Moon in the third, sixth, seventh, eighth, and twelfth are unfavorable. The Moon's placement in the second, fourth, fifth, ninth, tenth, and eleventh are all good—but this is not the case if the Moon is ultimately judged to be a malefic. Indeed, one line of thought has it that all the planets are good in the eleventh, even if they are malefics. Some say this is the case unless they happen to be in debilitation or combust when in the eleventh house. I concur with this view. Moon's placement in the ascendant is generally unfavorable.

MOON IN LAGNA. If lagna is Aries, Moon there is good and will produce progeny. If lagna is Taurus, the Moon there will produce wealth, and this applies to a Cancer ascendant as well. Moon in the other signs in the ascendant is conducive to the mode of ignorance.

MOON IN THE SECOND: A large family is indicated.

MOON IN THE THIRD: Mischievous or even murderous tendencies.

MOON IN THE FOURTH: Happiness and houses.

MOON IN THE FIFTH: Sons and good intelligence.

MOON IN THE SIXTH: Enemies.

MOON IN THE SEVENTH: Jealousy in a life full of passion.

MOON IN THE EIGHTH: Illness and anxiety.

MOON IN THE NINTH: Fortune and prosperity.

MOON IN THE TENTH: Success, wealth, and heroism.

MOON IN THE ELEVENTH: Fame and profit.

MOON IN THE TWELFTH: Defective limbs and evil acts.

Moon is a benefic when waxing and a malefic when waning, previous to judging him according to house lordship. However, when in the first tithi of the waxing paksha, Moon is combust and still a malefic. The process of reconciliation and final determination requires fine discrimination, so as not to get bogged down by apparent contradictions. Of course, a planet often *does* produce contradictory indicators as per his sign versus house placement; a human being is constitutionally a very complex entity. Try to blend the descriptions of each placement and let the resultant emerge.

Results can be auspicious, evil, or mixed. Any exalted planet will only give good results; even if his house readings do not indicate such results, the exalted planet nullifies all those indicators.

If a planet is in Mula-Trikona, that will nullify three-quarters of the negative qualities indicated by sign or house placement. A planet in his own house nullifies half and empowers half. A planet in a friend's house nullifies a quarter of the bad reading. A planet in his enemy's or great enemy's sign is worse. A debilitated planet and a combust planet indicate inauspicious results (unless neecha-bhanga applies to the debilitation). These are the overall guides to judgment at octave two of this science.

SUN IN ARIES: Very good; place of exaltation. Fame, dexterity, craftiness, military opportunities, wealth, ability.

SUN IN TAURUS: Mixed. Makes livelihood with feminine items but dislikes females generally. Skilled in music and song.

SUN IN GEMINI: Good. Learned in many subjects, include astrology, literature, and poetry. Wealthy.

SUN IN CANCER: Bad. Irritable, fierce, poor, engages in hard labor, and prone to fatigue.

SUN IN LEO: Good; own sign. Lover of mountainous and forested regions. Powerful with high thoughts but not very literate.

SUN IN VIRGO: Meticulous fault-finder; similar to Sun in Gemini but not as good. Often inclined toward homosexuality (check other factors).

SUN IN LIBRA: Very bad; sign of debilitation. Engages in intoxication, low service, and aimless wandering.

SUN IN SCORPIO: Mixed. Adventurous and daring. Skilled in martial arts. Earnings through selling poisonous and similar items.

SUN IN SAGITTARIUS: Good. Appreciated by good people, wealthy, perceptive, intelligent, and artistic. Sometimes inclined toward medical activities.

SUN IN CAPRICORN: Bad. Avaricious and opportunistic. Exploitative; low mercantile activities. Possesses above-average wealth, but evil, mean, inarticulate, and not very literate.

SUN IN AQUARIUS: Bad. His actions will be below his eligibility. He will lose his son and wealth, winding up poor.

SUN IN PISCES: Good. Fortune obtained by selling products from rivers and oceans while accruing honor; receives feminine love.

SUN IN LAGNA: If Aries, this is conducive to wealth. If Leo, he will not possess night vision, but on the whole it is a good house for the Sun. If Libra, he will be poor and could become blind. If Cancer, there will be eye trouble. In all of the other signs, Sun in lagna makes a person brave, heroic, but also slow and dull.

SUN IN SECOND: Wealth is generated but plundered by the government; there could be some kind of mouth disease.

SUN IN THIRD: This makes one intelligent and powerful.

SUN IN FOURTH: It creates mental disturbances and unhappiness.

SUN IN FIFTH: No children and money is confiscated.

SUN IN SIXTH: It makes a person strong but he is still often conquered.

SUN IN SEVENTH: Trouble from women; controlled by women.

SUN IN EIGHTH: Defective eyes; unfavorable for progeny.

SUN IN NINTH: Wealth, progeny, and happiness.

SUN IN TENTH: Makes a person strong and happy.

SUN IN ELEVENTH: Conducive for great attainment of wealth.

SUN IN TWELFTH: It degrades and ruins a man.

The Sun is a great benefic in Aries, a benefic in its own sign, and a neutral in Sagittarius and Pisces. It is a malefic in all the other signs.

MARS IN ARIES and MARS IN SCORPIO: Good; own signs. He will receive honor from rulers, become a commander, and will like to travel. It is conducive for wealth. He will get permanent scars. He will gain possessions and enjoy sensually. There is a proclivity toward thievery.

MARS IN TAURUS and MARS IN LIBRA: Bad. He will come under the control of women and alienate his friends. There are illicit connections.

He will be good at magic. He will like fine clothing and will be timid. He will speak roughly and not be affectionate.

MARS IN GEMINI and MARS IN VIRGO: Mixed. He will be a spirited individual and will do good for others. He will be clever in singing and understand how music works. He will be fearless and aggressive. He will secure his money. He will likely have an issue. He will be intolerant and will not make friends easily. He will be a miser.

MARS IN CANCER: Very bad; sign of debilitation. Despite this fact, the reading is actually mixed. He will be cruel, wicked, deceitful, and have a pronounced bodily defect. But he will also be rich, learned, and earn money through overseas ventures or items of the seas.

MARS IN LEO: Bad. This placement produces endurance, but it also produces poverty, wandering (particularly in forests), and it is not favorable for family life.

MARS IN SAGITTARIUS and MARS IN PISCES: Good. Favorable for political advancement, reputation, fearlessness, and progeny. But it does create many enemies in the process.

MARS IN AQUARIUS: Bad. Misery, wealth deprivation, lying, wandering, and an idiosyncratic temperament.

MARS IN CAPRICORN: Very good. This is his sign of exaltation. A person with this placement lives like a king; favorable for wealth creation. As far as the house readings for Mars are concerned, they are exactly similar to the readings for the Sun with these exceptions:

MARS IN LAGNA: There will be marks from wounds on the body.

MARS IN SECOND: A person will eat bitter, harsh, or coarse meals.

MARS IN NINTH: This indicates sinful activities.

Mars is a benefic in his sign of exaltation and in his own signs. He is a malefic in all the other signs. If he is the lord of both a quadrant and a trine, he can give only good results as the chart's yogakaraka.

MERCURY IN ARIES and MERCURY IN SCORPIO: Bad. This placement makes a person gamble, go into debt, become a drunkard, an atheist, a thief, and poverty-stricken. He will be a big sense enjoyer, and will also be a liar as well as arrogant.

MERCURY IN TAURUS and MERCURY IN LIBRA: Good. This sign placement makes a person speak of higher knowledge, liberal, devoted to advanced personalities, and intent on earning. He will be successful in the matter of wives and children.

MERCURY IN GEMINI: Good; own sign. He will be expert at detailing ironies, learned in scripture, proficient in the fine arts, sweet in speech, and fond of luxury and comfort.

MERCURY IN CANCER: Mixed. This person will become inimical to his friends and relatives and will earn money through the sales of goods connected to the ocean.

MERCURY IN LEO: Bad. He will be readily disliked, hated by women, almost an illiterate, and a wanderer. He will lose his money, children, and honor. He will be lusty and unhappy.

MERCURY IN VIRGO: Very good. This is his sign of exaltation, Mula Trikona, and his own sign as well. He will be scholarly, forgiving, happy, unselfish, and generous. He will be fearless and able to persuade others.

MERCURY IN CAPRICORN and MERCURY IN AQUARIUS: Bad. He will constantly be engaged as a servant and often unpaid for that service. He will fall into debt. He will have some sculpting talent.

MERCURY IN SAGITTARIUS: Good. He will be honored by political leaders. He will be learned, especially the legal and astrological sciences.

MERCURY IN PISCES: Very bad. Mercury is debilitated here, but the reading is mixed nevertheless. He will be a very low servant, but he will stay loyal to his service. He will be a good friend and listener; intelligent. Mercury has exactly the same reading in some of his house placements as does the Sun; you can consult those to advantage. Here are the others:

MERCURY IN LAGNA: A person becomes learned.

MERCURY IN SECOND: Conducive to wealth.

MERCURY IN THIRD: Wickedness.

MERCURY IN FOURTH: A person becomes learned.

MERCURY IN FIFTH: Inclines one to ecclesiastic orders.

MERCURY IN SIXTH: A person is without enemies.

MERCURY IN SEVENTH: A man of virtue and/or a lawyer.

MERCURY IN EIGHTH: Conducive to fame and good qualities.

Mercury is generically a benefic except when debilitated, combust, or conjunct a malefic. When conjunct Sun, however, Mercury is not made a malefic; as long as he is not combust, a favorable yoga is produced. Mercury conjunct Sun produces the auspicious Budha-Aditya Yoga, conducive to learning and enlightenment. Mercury can be made into a malefic due to house lordship, of course.

JUPITER IN ARIES and JUPITER IN SCORPIO: Good. He commands with authority and obtains much wealth. He has a good wife and sons. He is generous and serves his fellow man. He is forgiving, dignified, and endowed with fine qualities. His wife is feisty.

JUPITER IN TAURUS and JUPITER IN LIBRA: Good. He will rarely fall ill, having a strong and stout body. He will be vigorous and attract wealth. He will be unselfish, charitable, admired, and well-liked. He will have many friends and sons.

JUPITER IN GEMINI and JUPITER IN VIRGO: Good. He will be a happy, ecclesiastic type. Nevertheless, he will possess houses, wives, sons, friends, servants, and excellent apparel.

JUPITER IN CANCER and JUPITER IN AQUARIUS: Very good; Canceer is sign of exaltation. He will be intelligent, prosperous, happy, and possess much property. He obtains wife, sons, and jewelry; influential.

JUPITER IN LEO: Good. He will be some kind of commander. The rest of the reading is similar to Jupiter in exaltation but not as good.

JUPITER IN SAGITTARIUS and JUPITER IN PISCES: Good; own signs. He will become head of his group and always attain political ascendancy. He will assist powerful politicians, eventually becoming an influential director himself.

JUPITER IN CAPRICORN: Very bad. This is his sign of debilitation. He will engage in vile acts below his level of eligibility. He will remain below the poverty line. There will be a great deal of misery in his life. Jupiter is good in all signs except Capricorn. Jupiter is also good in nine out of twelve house placements, although this will only be the case if he is not converted into a malefic due to house lordship. A well-placed benefic Jupiter in a quadrant or a trine is most helpful in any chart; it mitigates a host of afflictions and obstacles.

JUPITER IN LAGNA: A person becomes very learned.

JUPITER IN SECOND: Sweet speech.

JUPITER IN THIRD: Miserliness.

JUPITER IN FOURTH: Great happiness.

JUPITER IN FIFTH: Very intelligent and generally victorious in argument.

JUPITER IN SIXTH: A person should be without enemies.

JUPITER IN SEVENTH: He surpasses his father in good qualities.

JUPITER IN EIGHTH: Low and mean activities.

JUPITER IN NINTH: Very austere and devoted to the Absolute Truth.

JUPITER IN TENTH: Great wealth through occupational success.

JUPITER IN ELEVENTH: Great profit easily attained.

JUPITER IN TWELFTH: Evil deeds invoking great fear in others.

VENUS IN ARIES and VENUS IN SCORPIO: Bad. Loss of property due to illicit connections with others' spouses, bringing much disgrace.

VENUS IN TAURUS and VENUS IN LIBRA: Good; own signs. A person makes a livelihood through his own prowess; he lives by his wits. He will be respected by political leaders. He will be fearless and become famous. He will always work his way to the top of his group.

VENUS IN GEMINI: Good. Engaged well in the political order, he will be wealthy and expert in music, very much liking to sing and dance.

VENUS IN CANCER: Bad. This placement makes a person avaricious, cowardly, lusty, and miserable; a cheating heart when it comes to romance.

VENUS IN LEO: Mixed. He will make his way in life via liaisons with women, eventually marrying and glorifying his wife. Limited progeny.

VENUS IN SAGITTARIUS: Good. He will be honored, possess many dignified qualities, and he will become wealthy.

VENUS IN CAPRICORN and VENUS IN AQUARIUS: Mixed. He will be handsome, popular, influenced by women, and engage in illicit connections. He will be attracted to low-class women.

VENUS IN PISCES: Very good; place of exaltation. Venus here will make him wealthy, learned, poised, dignified, and endowed with good qualities. The placement also favors an acting career or professional singing.

VENUS IN VIRGO: Very bad. Debilitated. A person born with this combination will engage constantly in labor that will consist of low and menial services.

VENUS IN LAGNA: Fondness for comfort and love.

VENUS IN FIFTH: Happiness.

VENUS IN SEVENTH: This makes a person a libertine and quarrelsome. For Venus' other house placement readings from the second through the twelfth, consult the readings given for Jupiter. Venus is generally a benefic in a chart, particularly when he is the yogakarka. However, negative house lordship can make him a malefic.

SATURN IN ARIES: Very bad. This is his sign of debilitation. This placement makes a person a fool, illiterate, a wanderer, and very deceptive. No one can remain his friend.

SATURN IN SCORPIO: Bad. A similar reading to the above-mentioned, only not quite as terrible.

SATURN IN TAURUS: Bad. This produces illicit sexual connections with low-class women, poverty, and multiple divorces.

SATURN IN GEMINI and SATURN IN VIRGO: Bad. This makes a man shameless, poverty-stricken, miserable, and without issue. He is prone to make mistakes in his writing and is not very literate. However, if he is in a prison, police, or security setting, he becomes an important officer there.

SATURN IN CANCER: Bad. Poverty and ever-decaying teeth which fall out are part of this karma; the teeth that remain are defective. He will lose his mother and sons. He will not be very literate.

SATURN IN LEO: Bad. This placement makes a person dishonored and unhappy. He will be illiterate, deprived of his sons, and he will always have to work as a peon.

SATURN IN CAPRICORN and SATURN IN AQUARIUS: Mixed. Surprisingly, these are the planet's own signs but the reading is nevertheless mixed; the reading in Aquarius is the better of the two. Wealth will be steady throughout life, and the person will enjoy what he acquires. He will secure wealth from other people by various means. He will prosper in the military or similar fields. He will have illicit connections. He will be dirty and vulgar. He will emerge as the director of his tribe.

SATURN IN SAGITTARIUS and SATURN IN PISCES: Good. He will remain conscious while dying. He will gain the confidences of political leaders while living. He will have a good wife and progeny. He will attain great wealth, eminence, and at the very least be a leader of his community.

SATURN IN LIBRA: Very good; sign of exaltation. He will be honored and will the chief of any assembly he joins. He will become very wealthy. As far as the house readings for Saturn (he is the son of the Sun) are concerned, except for in the ascendant, they are the same as those readings for the Sun in all of his houses placements.

SATURN IN ARIES IN LAGNA: A person is afflicted by chronic illnesses beginning in childhood. He is dirty, poor, and lusty. This same reading applies when the ascendant is **TAURUS, GEMINI, CANCER, LEO, VIRGO, and SCORPIO.**

SATURN IN LIBRA IN LAGNA: Authority, learning, and beautiful appearance. This same reading applies when the ascendant is **CAPRICORN, AQUARIUS, and PISCES.**

Saturn is generically a malefic unless he is exalted, in his own houses, or in the eleventh house. If he is the lord of both a quadrant and a trine, he will give only good results as the yogakaraka; these good results might come in rather unpleasant ways, however. Yogakaraka is the best planet.

Overall judgment is based upon many factors. The presence of another planet in the same house with any given planet will modify his reading. If he is a neutral, his presence in an enemy's or great enemy's sign will turn him into a malefic. A planet will sometimes be turned into a malefic if conjunct a malefic; this is all the more so when two or more planets are in conjunction with him in any given house. Obviously he will become, if a generic benefic, a much greater benefic if conjunct benefics.

If a planet in a given house is in his friendly sign, it magnifies the good reading in that house. An exalted planet mitigates all that is a bad reading for that house and maximizes all that is favorable in relation to the house interpretation, even if that is only a small part of his reading.

An auspicious or benefic planet in any good house is helpful to the horoscope. A benefic is often a bit helpful when placed in bad houses. Usually a benefic even in the twelfth will decrease losses, expenditures, hospital stays, secret enemies, and insanity. Usually a benefic in the sixth will tamp down the creation of known enemies. Malefics in these houses produce opposite results. One line of thought cringes at a malefic's placement in a bad house. However, if a malefic is in a bad house, that means it is not damaging any of the good houses. From that perspective, you would prefer to have your malefics in bad houses.

You should not get lost in meticulous or superfluous details that surround much of what passes today for sidereal astrology. There are many software programs offering voluminous minutiae, interpretations, and options connected to the planets, the signs, the life stages, the aspects, etc. The vast majority of all of these are ultimately little more than rabbit holes; diving into them will get you entangled in endless contradictions and diversions. This study of sidereal astrology at octave two is not meant for that.

Chapter Six

MOON IN THE NAKSHATRAS

Varahamihira in the <u>Brihaj-jataka</u> includes a separate chapter on the Moon in the nakshatras or constellations; I shall follow in his footsteps. Judgments in sidereal astrology are attained by judicious blending or interpretation of overlapping influences in connection to both the lunar sign and nakshatra.

Every nakshatra has its own nature, own gana, and own lord. In my experience, the lords of the nakshatras are not important in terms of interpretation. As such, I am not even going to list them. The nature and the gana of the constellations are very important as far as interpretation is concerned.

The nature can be one of seven: Light, dreadful, mixed, fixed, soft, sharp, or movable. The gana is one of three: Deva, manushya, or rakshasa. This is essential knowledge. Deva means godly. Manushya means human (basically, in the mode of passion). Rakshasa means diabolical. These two categories, viz., nature and gana, are presented with each reading.

MOON IN ASHVINI: This is a light-natured constellational position for the Moon. It is deva gana, as well. The person likes to display his or her clothes and ornaments. He or she has an engaging personality and is often very good looking. He or she is playfully sneaky and clever, developing outstanding and fine skills. He or she is endowed with a better-than-average intelligence but does not always use it.

MOON IN BHARANI: Nature: Dreadful. Gana: Manushya. The person develops a very firm resolve when Moon is here. He is good at what he does. He is generally truthful, happy, generally healthy, and does not lament.

MOON IN KRITTIKA: Nature: Mixed. Gana: Rakshasa. This person is a big eater, engages in illicit sexual connections, is intolerant, and very attached to name and fame. He or she has a feisty nature, also.

MOON IN ROHINI: Nature: Fixed. Gana: Human (manushya). This makes a person very smooth in a persuasive way. He is clean, truthful, not covetous, attentive to his appearance, and very reliable.

MOON IN MRIGASHIRA: Nature: Soft. Gana: Godly (deva). The person is quick and fleeting whenever the situation requires it. Ingenuity and skill are intrinsic to his repertoire. He is very much into taste tests. He is active, rich, and hopeful—but also a bit timid.

MOON IN ARDRA: Nature: Sharp. Gana: Human. This man is vicious, deceptive, likes intrigues, vain, and is often harmful to others.

MOON IN PUNARVASU: Nature: Movable. Gana: Godly. This person has forebearance, controls his passions, is happy, polite, a bit dull (contrary to the Gemini nature in general, if the Moon is on that side), gets sick often, is often thirsty and dissatisfied.

MOON IN PUSHYA: Nature: Light. Gana: Godly. This constellation is the best one of the twenty-seven. He is peaceful, has great control over sense gratification, is handsome, learned in the scriptures, observes religious rituals with diligence, likes ceremonies, and is wealthy.

MOON IN ASHLESHA: Nature: Sharp. Gana: Diabolical. He is dishonest, devours anything and everything, very crafty, and into intrigue, treachery, and betrayal. He readily engages in evil acts.

MOON IN MAGHA: Nature: Dreadful. Gana: Diabolical. The nature and the gana are not good, yet he is very enthusiastic in whatever he attempts, believing that the demigods and his forefathers will help him. He delights in sexual enjoyment, possessing both wealth and devoted attendants.

MOON IN PURVA PHALGUNI: Nature: Dreadful. Gana: Human. This is a very likable person, good looking, famous, and charitable. He is a wanderer. He kisses up to the powerful and politically prominent.

MOON IN UTTARA PHALGUNI: Nature: Fixed. Gana: Human. He pays attention to detail, earning money via literary pursuits. He is happy and is also very sensual.

MOON IN HASTA: Nature: Light. Gana: Godly. Despite the fact that this is a deva nakshatra, the reading here is mostly adverse. He gets intoxicated regularly; he is ruthless, reactionary, and has a tendency to thieve. He is bold and enthusiastic, even though this is a light nakshatra.

MOON IN CHITRA: Nature: Soft. Gana: Diabolical. This is the nakshatra of attractive elegance. He or she wears multi-colored decorations with good taste, especially in clothing. He or she possesses poise, charm, and a beautifully proportioned body. It is a very Venusian constellation, although half of it is in Virgo. It is not favorable for control of the senses.

MOON IN SVATI: Nature: Movable. Gana: Godly. This person is inclined toward mercantile affairs. He is merciful, sweet of speech, virtuous, and subdues his senses.

MOON IN VISHAKHA: Nature: Mixed. Gana: Diabolical. A mixed reading if found here, as per the nature. He is persuasive and speaks attractively. However, he is also envious, greedy, and can be very quarrelsome. He has a bright complexion and is clever in earning.

MOON IN ANURADHA: Nature: Soft. Gana: Godly. This person has difficulties with austerity and cannot endure hunger. He or she likes to travel and is attracted to new experiences and new places, especially foreign locations. Wealth is often obtained in connection to these travels.

MOON IN JYESTHA: Nature: Sharp. Gana: Diabolical. This presents another mixed reading. This person is contented and virtuous, but he is also very angry. As such, he has great difficulty making friends.

MOON IN MULA: Nature: Sharp. Gana: Diabolical. They demand respect; they command it as well. They secure wealth and are happy. They can concentrate their minds, and they gravitate toward a luxurious lifestyle.

MOON IN PURVASHADHA: Nature: Dreadful. Gana: Human. This man is proud. He is honored by everyone and is a reliable friend. He is comfortable, happy, and seeks out (and usually finds) a very favorable wife.

MOON IN UTTARASHADHA: Nature: Fixed. Gana: Human. This unblemished reading describes a man who is handsome, popular, always grateful, and religious. He acquiesces to authority. He is always a gentleman and, as such, has many friends.

MOON IN SHRAVANA: Nature: Movable. Gana: Godly. This is the second most auspicious constellation of the Moon (after Pushya). This person is learned in Vedic knowledge. He is fortunate and eventually prospers. He obtains wealth, honor, and has a special consort.

MOON IN DHANISTHA: Nature: Movable. Gana: Diabolical. He desires wealth constantly and obtains it. Charitable. Heroic and really likes music.

MOON IN SHATABHISHA: Nature: Movable. Gana: Diabolical. This man is bold, daring, and active. He is also generally harsh and vicious.

MOON IN PURVA BHADRAPADA: Nature: Dreadful. Gana: Human. He is tight-fisted. He obtains wealth, in no small part because he is clever in doing so. He is prone to be anxiety-ridden and subject to lamentation. He is always controlled by his wife.

MOON IN UTTARA BHADRAPADA: Nature: Fixed. Gana: Human. He likes to speak on religious topics and does so very nicely. He is religious. He overcomes his enemies; as such, he is happy. He is part of a long lineage of similar distinguished personalities.

MOON IN REVATI: Nature: Soft. Gana: Godly. There is a pure innocence found here. His body is powerfully built. He has poise and a kind of heroic grace. He obtains wealth usually without difficulty.

Let us recount the lunar nakshatras that are most favorable for wealth: Mrigasira, Pushya, Magha, Utttara Phalguni, Vishakha, Anuradha (circumstantially), Mula, Shravana, Dhanistha, Purva Bhadrapada, and Revati. In the descriptions of the Moon in the nakshatras, like all the other qualities or karmas predicting wealth (or any element in a horoscope), it requires a blending and thorough analysis of all influences in the chart.

Chapter Seven

BASIC SHAD-BALA

According to sidereal astrology, the chief determination of the strength of any of the seven major planets is secured via an analysis of shad-bala. There are six divisions of shad-bala. These six divisions are, in order of priority: 1) Sthana-bala, 2) Dig-bala, 3) Kala-bala, 4) Chestha-bala, 5) Yuddha-bala (infrequently applicable), and 6) Naisargika-bala. It can be a bit confusing, because the first bala, sthana-bala, is also divided into six different divisions. Its six divisions are referred to as shad-vargas.

The Sanskrit word *shad* means "six." In the sthana-*bala*—which is the first of six divisions comprising the aforementioned shad-bala (six balas or six different divisions of power or strength)—any given planet is obviously in a sign. The Sanskrit word for sign is *rashi*. That placement constitutes the first of the six divisions of sthana-bala. Besides being in a sign, a planet is also in subdivisions of that sign. There are many of them ultimately, but five are more prominent than the others: The *hora*, the *dreshkana* (decanate), the *navamsha*, the *dvadashamsha*, and the *trimshamsha*. To reiterate, these are called the shad-*vargas*, in order to distinguish them from shad-bala.

The hora constitutes one-half of the sign. It corresponds to our English word "hour," because, on average, it takes about one hour for any sign on the ascendant to pass from its first degree to its halfway point on the eastern horizon. Obviously, we are referring to the ascendant or lagna here. In every sign, either the Sun or the Moon rules one of these halves; the other five major planets have nothing to do with the hora. That is compensated for in the trimshamsha interpretation, however.

The lagna is made strong when occupied by its own ruler. It is also strengthened, but to a bit lesser degree, when aspected by its ruler. The ascendant is rendered strong when occupied by benefic Mercury or Jupiter, provided neither of them is combust. It becomes weakened when occupied by malefics, but not by any planet exalted there or in its own sign. Obviously, a planet is always in a hora whether it is in the lagna or in any of the other eleven houses.

After hora there is dreshkana, which is one-third of a sign. After that subdivision, there is the most important amsha (part or subdivision), and it is called the navamsha. Nava means "nine," and the na-vamsha is one-ninth of any given sign. The navamsha chart is a sepa-rate chart that all sidereal astrologers look to with keen interest while analyzing the natal chart. The point of the ascendant falls in a certain navamsha, and all the seven major planets are situated in their given navamshas. This creates another chart, with the navamsha covering lagna point becoming the new ascendant for that chart (if it's the same ascendant as the natal chart, that also makes the lagna stronger; it is called lagna vargottama).

Signs are made strong when they correspond to kendras. Hu-man signs are strong during the daytime, and animal signs are strong at night. Reptile signs are strong during twilight times.

After navamsha, we come to the subdivision known as dvada-shamsha; it is one-twelfth of a sign. As such, each dvadashamsha cor-responds to two minutes and thirty seconds of sidereal arc of any of the signs.

It is also mentioned that signs become strong or weak according to benefic or malefic aspects on those signs, but these influences are always secondary to the effect of planets actually occupying houses. The situation of calculating aspects for any given sign is rather tedious work.

Finally, there is the trimshamsha, which is one-thirtieth of a sign. Since all signs consist of thirty degrees of sidereal arc, each trim-shamsha ideally constitutes one degree. However, for practical appli-cation, it is a bit different. This difference makes it easier to accurately calculate the trimshamsha positions of any of the seven major planets in comparison to the navamsha or the dvadashamsha positions. As hinted at previously, the Sun and the Moon do not rule any trim-shamshas. The other five major planets rule the trimshamsha subdivi-sions, but they do not alternatively rule trimshamshas (alternating from one degree to the next); each of the five other planets rules a set of consecutive degrees in the odd and even signs.

I have provided detailed tables of all these subdivisions (of sthana-bala) in Appendix Two at the end of this book.

Having described sthana-bala and its six subdivisions, let us re-turn to the discussion of the overall shad-bala. To reiterate, sthana-bala comprises one-sixth of the six-fold shad-bala. Some sidereal as-trologers consider that aspects form a part of the shad-bala calcula-tion; I disagree.

In my experience, the effects of aspects are most noticeable when they are connected to planets within a particular aspect close to the same exact degree of their planetary placements. For example, a ninety-degree aspect from Saturn at seven degrees in one sign to a planet also at seven degrees of the other sign will show significant effect.

Tropical astrology places emphasis on applying and separating aspects; this traces back to the aforementioned tajjika system. Most of the rules of that system, however, apply only to that system. An over-emphasis on aspects in interpretation of natal or election charts is like beating a depleted husk of corn for a few kernels of nourishment.

There are many bewildering and contradictory indicators in all the translations of Vedic astrological texts. I have, even in these primary principles, simplified everything in order to avoid most of those controversies. This advanced primer is a straightforward presentation according to my realization. I make judgments according to my knowledge, understanding, and experience. If you are able to understand and accept what I give you here, then you will save energy, time, and counterproductive mental gyrations. I already previously went through all of that for you. You may also wind up saving money.

You may be able to make some money, as well.

You can use either the fixed friends-and-enemies standard or the temporary friends-and-enemies adjusted standard to calculate sthana-bala; my recommendation is to go with the modification, i.e., the adjusted status.

Shad-bala or six-fold strength has, as the term implies, six divisions that determine how strong or weak a planet is. One of these divisions, called yuddha-bala, is infrequently applicable. The other five are always present, but one of them is a fixed measurement of strength (naisargika-bala). The strength of lagna must also be calculated, but that is not done in the same way as the strength of the seven major planets are calculated in shad-bala.

This bala part of the science can be a bit controversial, so let us delve into it more fully (at second octave) in order to understand it better. If, for some of you, money is not an issue, you could actually check out what I am about to give as an example. There are wild variances in the calculation of shad-bala. Say you download onto your hard-drive ten sidereal programs, all of them sophisticated enough to include the shad-bala calculation for each of the seven major planets (none of the programs that I know of calculate strength of lagna). You then make a printout of your planetary shad-bala totals.

You are shocked to discover that not even two of them match. Over and above this, you find that there is a wide range or variance for these ten different shad-bala conclusions. You might decide to average out the shad-bala totals for each planet, believing that this step would give you a good idea of just how powerful or weak each of your planets actually is. That may not yield better results. In other words, in terms of the ten printouts, two of them might actually be reasonably close to accurate; averaging all ten might take you further away from the reality.

In my sidereal instruction course, I'll give you my system, i.e., the point tallies (rupas) that I use. As mentioned previously, one of the shad-bala calculations, known as yuddha-bala, does not come into play very often at all. When it does, a determination has to be made to score it. There is a fixed order of calculation in one of the balas (nai-sargika-bala); that is accepted by everyone and is not controversial. I'll tell you how I score it if and/or when you decide to become a C.O.R.E. sidereal astrologer.

So, that leaves four more shad-balas to discuss. Two of those are not very controversial; their calculations are generally straightforward, with some minor exceptions. Two of the others are controversial.

The fixed bala is known as naisargika-bala. I list it first here, although Varahamihira lists it last. It is the same for everybody. I assign the maximum rupas for the topmost planet in naisargika-bala, which happens to be the Sun. Next most powerful is the Moon, followed by Venus, Jupiter, Mercury, Mars, and finally Saturn. Saturn has about one-sixth of the power of the Sun as per naisargika-bala. I grade these planets to scale.

Then we come to sthana-bala. This is the most important of the shad-balas or six divisions of strength. Sthana means placement. If the correct ayanamsha is employed, the planets will accurately be found to occupy different subdivisions of a sign. Of course, a planet's placement in its proper sign is ultra-important. I give more weight to sthana-bala than I do for each of the other four subdivisions of strength (yuddha-bala is calculated in a completely different way).

Sthana-bala is one of six balas, and sthana-bala itself has within itself six different divisions. These six, as previously mentioned, are called the rashi, the hora, the dreshkana, the navamsha, the dvadasamsha, and the trimsamsha. I do not give these subdivisions equal weight in my system. I give the navamsha more weight than the other subdivisions, and I give the placement of the planet in the sign the most weight.

In other words, I calculate the sthana-bala according to scale. As a rough average, because there are so many possible permutations, I have assigned a maximum of twice as many rupas to sthana-bala for a given planet in comparison to the maximum for any of the other balas. With extraordinarily propitious placements, some planets could score above this total. It is almost impossible to pinpoint what the average would be in sthana-bala. It merits more rupas than does dig-bala, chestha-bala, kala-bala, or naisargika-bala. An exalted planet in a sign is going to attain the most rupas possible, but an exalted planet in navamsha is going to tally the same rupas as a planet in Mula Trikona or its own sign.

After sthana-bala, we proceed to dig-bala or directional strength. Like sthana-bala, its calculation is proportional. Say, for example, Jupiter is very close to the point of lagna. That is generally an excellent placement, as long as he is not debilitated or combust there. Let us put Saturn in the second for a further illustration of the principle. Jupiter is going to attain almost full dig-bala or maximum rupas. Jupiter in the ascendant is his best position in terms of his particular dig-bala.

However, Saturn gets his full dig-bala in the seventh. In this hypothetical chart, Saturn is almost exactly opposite his best position for directional strength. Saturn would attain only a minimum number of rupas.

Jupiter and Mercury achieve peak dig-bala in the ascendant. Sun and Mars get it in the tenth, Saturn in the seventh, and the Moon and Venus achieve peak dig-bala in the fourth house. They get no dig-bala when positioned exactly opposite these placements.

Then there is kala-bala. It is the time strength. Like sthana-bala, there are also six subdivisions to kala-bala. Each of the planets either attains the maximum allotted to the subdivision or gets no rupas for non-attainment. In the case of four (of these six) subdivisions, only one planet attains the maximum and all the other planets get shut out.

For example, I give more weight to the planet that was the lord of the hour than I give to the planet that was the lord of the year; this determination is made on the basis of concentrated time. The day/night subdivision of kala-bala is fixed. If it was a night birth, then

Moon, Mars, and Saturn attain the rupas allotted. If it was a day birth, then the Sun, Jupiter, and Venus attain it. Mercury automatically attains kala-bala. The paksha subdivision is also fixed; this relates to whether or not the Moon is waxing or waning. If waxing, the benefics attain the allotted rupas (remember, an exalted planet is always a benefic). If the Moon was waning, the malefics attain this subdivision's rupas.

The lord of the year, month, day, and hour are automatically calculated by any quality sidereal program. However, beware of a glitch I have noticed. Sometimes programs start at midnight for determining the astrological day. This is wrong, as the day starts *astrologically* at sunrise. If a birth commenced after midnight but before the upcoming sunrise, then the lord of the day still reigns from the previous sunrise—and that would be on the previous date. You have to double-check this one.

Then we come to the really controversial bala, namely the chestha-bala. In Sanskrit, the word chestha is described in the dictionary as meaning "motion or movement." Some consider it to mean "brightness" also. Virtually all post-modern siderealists interpret it to mean "speed."

A planet is always in motion. For example, as per declination, a planet may be in its northern course or its southern course. Similarly, a planet may be in motion conjunct one or two other planets; it may be in motion where it is moving toward or away from another planet. It may be in direct or forward motion. It may be in retrograde motion.

The text in Brihaj-jataka describing what constitutes chestha-bala attaining or not attaining is both cryptic and succinct. Most importantly, there is no follow-through on this particular subdivision of strength anywhere else in Varahamihira's book. As a counter-example, in relation to benefics and malefics, there are (a few) further modifications and clarifications presented. This is not afforded to the description of chestha-bala, however.

As such, I simply accept the terse description with a straightforward interpretation, not seeking to clarify or modify it in any way. I accept the direct meaning. The text says that the Sun attains chestha-bala when it is in its northern course; you can calculate this proportionately using the rule of three, i.e., Sun would get full chestha-bala in early June. Similarly, the text says that Moon attains chestha-bala when it is in its northern course.

The rule for chestha-bala further states that any retrograde planet receives it. Its *movement* is retrograde. Finally, the text says that any planet or planets conjunct Moon receives chestha-bala. Do planets conjunct Moon move more slowly? I do not know that to be true.

Finally, we come to the sixth bala of shad-bala. It is called yuddha-bala or planetary war. It only attains when two planets are located in the same degree of any given sign. It must be calculated last. The planet that is northward in declination wins the battle. In my system, I give the winner half of the accumulated rupas from the planet defeated in this war. Even if in a more southerly direction, however, Venus is always the victor in any yuddha-bala. Yuddha-bala never applies to the Sun or Moon.

Now let us proceed to the important calculation of the strength of lagna or the ascendant. After pondering this in terms of the Brihajjataka—and in conjunction with my experience—I have gleaned these twelve prominent factors in order to attain this determination:

1) power is attained by lagna automatically, since it is both a kendra and a trine simultaneously,

2) power is attained when either benefic Mercury or Jupiter is in the ascendant (what to speak of both of them—but only as benefics),

3) the strength of the lord of lagna, or his weakness, factors into this calculation,

4) if the lord of the ascendant powerfully aspects the lagna, that promotes the ascendant's power,

5) the lagna automatically gets more power when it is a human sign,

6) an exalted planet in lagna accentuates its power,

7) lagna power is increased if it was a day sign during a day birth or a night sign during a night birth,

8) if at night the lagna was Aries, Taurus, Leo, or Sagittarius (animal signs), it gets empowerment,

9) a powerful and benefic aspect from benefic Mercury or Jupiter or any benefic makes it more powerful,

10) power is taken away from the lagna when a malefic is situated in it,

11) power is taken away when a debilitated planet is there,

12) power is granted when the lagna is vargottama (described above).

Determining a potential for total rupas that matches the other planets is necessary, because lagna can be stronger or weaker than any other planet. If it is stronger than the Sun and Moon, the first dasha will commence with the lagna dasha. Calculating lagna strength is as essential as calculating the strengths individually of the other seven major planets. You should be able to clearly see by now that determining the strengths of the seven major planets and lagna is intricate. Formulating this system involves an organized format. Currently, there are no accurate software programs that do the work—none that I know of. As such, you or your astrologer has to make the calculations. You need to commit many things to memory and consult the tables provided. You have to get all of the steps in the right order.

This chapter would not be complete if it did not include a breakdown of some of the most common foibles connected to shadbala. In relation to sthana-bala, there should be no *separate* ucchabala—there should be no separate calculation of an exalted planet as a bala unto itself. Exalted planets should be accorded the highest number of rupas as per which subdivision they are found to be exalted in sthana-bala. There are six divisions of shad-bala, not seven.

Prominence must be separated from power. A planet is more *prominent* when it is in a quadrant; it is more *powerful* when it is in a favorable sign. Shad-*bala* is the calculation of *power*, not prominence. Sometimes, you will find software that makes a separate calculation for ayana bala; that should be part of the kala-bala interpretation, however. The Sun and Moon also attain chestha-bala when they are in their northern courses (ayana refers to either the northern or southern course). Sometimes, kala-bala is broken down into seven subdivisions instead of six; that is but another concoction.

Chapter Eight

DASHAS

The purpose of dashas is to ascertain the actual periods of your life, your life stages, as well as to ascertain your scheduled length of life. Even though only preliminaries of the dasha methods will be provided in this chapter, some people or readers will still find the particulars overwhelming. Trust me when I tell you that I had to wade through that same problem, and it took me years. However, once you get the system (or, you could say, three systems) down, it is not overwhelmingly difficult to comprehend and apply.

In both the Brihat Parashara Hora, as well as in the Brihaj-jataka, these dashas are primarily determined by one of three systems or methods: The pindayu method, the nisargayu method, or the amshayu method. However, both of the aforementioned texts are very old. Over time, methods or systems that were once well-established — facts and truths that were understood by virtually everyone — become changed.

The system known as the vimshottari dasha method is also mentioned in the BPH; it is not mentioned at all in the Brihaj-jataka. It is obviously not nearly as important (for determining the actual dashas) as the abovementioned three systems. Nevertheless, it is now practically the only dasha system employed by post-modern sidereal astrologers.

The Nineteenth Century seems like a very long time ago. In one sense it is. In the West as of 2009, there are hardly any people still living that were born in or around that epoch. There are still fewer that have any kind of remote memory of it. However, we must also consider it in terms of scale. According to how long the sidereal science has been extant on Earth, that timeframe was very recent.

As aforementioned, virtually every siderealist throughout the world employs what is called the vimshottari dasha system in order to delineate and interpret the major life stages in an individual horoscope. If you have ever had your sidereal chart done, then you know of this system. It's based upon the idea that your first major dasha began according to which nakshatra your Moon was situated in at the time of birth.

In other words, every complete nakshatra corresponds to a certain planetary dasha of a fixed length of years. These planetary dashas, when added together, comprise one hundred and twenty years of life (then you return to the nakshatra you started from). In this vimshottari system, you begin at some place in a certain dasha (you have passed through it to some extent), and then the order of the rest of your dashas is fixed after that.

However, back in the Eighteenth Century, sidereal astrologers in Bengal (the headquarters of astrology in India), were not employing it very much at all. At that time, the three dasha systems mentioned at the top of this chapter were calculated, not vimshottari. Those three systems are complicated calculations. They involve many computations and considerations that require judgment, interpretation, and ordering. They all indicate a fixed duration of life. The vimshottari is very easy to calculate, does not required complicated determinations, and has no fixed duration.

The duration of life in vimshottari is guessed at in various ways. According to that system, many of its dashas afford some way or other to consider it potentially as the last dasha of a person's life. This is because there are, even in the best of charts, at least three or four planets that are conducive to death. The lords of the second and seventh houses (for a Libra ascendant, it is only one planet) are called marakas or planets which cause death. The lord of the twelfth is also considered to be like them, to a lesser extent. Any planet in the twelfth can serve this purpose as well.

So, in vimshottari, there are many dashas that can be considered dangerous.

In the vimshottari system, there are major dashas (also sometimes called mula dashas) and antardashas; the antardashas are sub-dashas within the major dasha. Those sub-periods (antardashas) may be ruled by marakas. As such, almost every mula dasha has some place or places in it that could facilitate a prediction of death.

In other words, even the very best dashas (major dashas) have intervals in them where a sidereal astrologer employing vimshottari could interpret the likelihood or possibility of death. This kind of leeway for interpretation is conducive to bluffing and fudging. The pindayu, nisargayu, and amsayu methods—hardly used by anyone these days—do not have this kind of elasticity of interpretation. In 1912, here's what Swami Vijnanananda had to say about the vimshottari method:

72

"The division of life into Dashas, as given by the author (Vara-hamihira), is hardly studied by the Indian astrologers, evidently from the difficulties in its application . . . The vimshottari system is nowadays finding its way into Bengal, too."

In order to become proficient at calculating the pindayu, nisargayu, and amshayu methods, training is advisable. In comparison to calculating the life stages via these three, vimshottari is a piece of cake. You can learn vimshottari just by studying any decent sidereal book that describes it; the system is simple. Over and above this, vimshottari is automatically included in all sidereal software and in most printouts. My advice, however, is to completely reject it right from the gate.

For one thing, there will automatically be a great disparity between two vimshottari printouts based upon the different ayanamshas that are programmed into the software. The position of the Moon may have shifted well over one or even two degrees due to this discrepancy. That would translate into a very different starting point as per the initial dasha; everything would be thrown off accordingly after that.

Secondly, once you believe something, you tend to turn it into some kind of "reality" for yourself. Vimshottari will give you a false set of assumptions in almost all cases. When those delusions become so entrenched that you rationalize contradictory indicators, you'll get stuck there.

You are receiving here an astrological foundation at the second level, what I call octave two. No one should jump to trigonometry before mastering addition, subtraction, multiplication, division, algebra, and geometry. All the rules and calculations governing the pindayu, nisargayu, and amshayu methods of Varahamihira are intricate—but they can be learned. All of them have an order depending upon the accuracy of the previous calculations, as well as proper application via correct comparative judgments.

I explain all of this to you in the comprehensive instructional course, but there is no completely accurate software representing these three methods to help you—none that I am aware of—at this time.

Now, each of these three systems has many identical and overlapping features. In other words, all three of them have a lot in common. However, they also have major differences between and amongst them; pindayu and nisargayu are more similar to each other than they are to amshayu. The planetary strength of the seven major planets (plus lagna) must first be determined in all three methods. We have discussed this in a previous chapter. Then, the order of the dashas is ascertained from those strengths. However, one of the systems must first be selected.

If the Sun is stronger than either Moon or the lagna, then you select the pindayu method. If Moon is the strongest of the three, then you go with the nisargayu method. If lagna is stronger than the Sun or Moon, your dasha method will be according to the amshayu system.

In this system (amshayu), there are seven planets that contribute a dasha to the total, and lagna makes the eighth contribution. Any malefic in the twelfth contributes no duration of life, so sometimes all eight durations or life stages are not part of the package. The determination is made from a final judgment as to whether any given planet (in the twelfth) is a malefic.

In the amshayu method, a malefic in the twelfth contributes zero days of life, but that's not entirely negative. That dasha, whatever it might otherwise have been in length, would have been very miserable. For the method of determining benefics and malefics (at octave two), consult the previous chapter which details a preliminary process of judgment.

Now, after it has been ascertained which of the seven planets (plus lagna) contribute a dasha (usually all eight of them), then their *order* must be calculated. Returning to a consideration of all three systems, the first dasha will either be the Sun, the Moon, or the lagna; the one of these that is the strongest will represent the first stage or duration of life. Shad-bala for each planet must be ascertained in order to make this determination, of course.

Some believe that the house of the strongest planet should be considered equivalent to lagna—that would mean a solar lagna or a lunar lagna (unless they are already in a kendra). They make its sign (if not in a kendra) a temporary kendra. As an example, let us say that you calculate (via shad-bala) that Moon is the strongest planet in the chart—stronger than the ascendant as well. So, Moon is in some house in your chart; they would make that house lagna (if not already a kendra) for the purpose of the nisargayu method. As you will see, the natal lagna of your actual horoscope, as well as all the other six major planets, have a specific house relationship to this Moon. Remember, this is nothing but a theoretical chart.

74

All planets (including lagna) that are in a quadrant from that Moon or conjunct that Moon will be part of the first dasha order. The Moon will be the initial dasha, and the other planets will follow in terms of their strength, the stronger planets first, the weaker after that.

The total dasha proceeds with planets in succedent houses (2, 5, 8, and 11) from the Moon under this principle; it would also include natal lagna. The planets (including lagna) in cadent houses (3, 6, 9, and 12) would finish it.

I do not accept this system. I apply the order based upon actual lagna and planetary positions in houses (succedent, cadent) accordingly; the only exception would be the planet representing the first dasha, if he is not already situated in a kendra.

Once the order has been ascertained, the duration of each dasha must be calculated. There is some math involved here, but it is all addition, subtraction, multiplication, and division. First of all, the importance of an accurate ayanamsha cannot be minimized in this connection, especially in relation to the amshayu method. That is because some of the planets are going to get their durations either increased or decreased (in amsayu only) based upon their placements in various subdivisions in the amshayu method. As such, an inaccurate navamsha will lead to divergent dasha lengths by not reproducing the actual subdivision in which the planet is situated.

Before obtaining the total life duration, the basic calculation of a given planetary dasha (and the lagna dasha) must be ascertained. This is the essence of the amshayu method, which I shall now describe. Every planet has a navamsha location, obviously. All the navamsha locations can be traced back to a most recent Aries navamsha (sometimes, the planet will be in Aries navamsha, obviously) in that series. According to this *basic* calculation, the first calculation, each navamsha (when completed) contributes one year of life. For example, if a planet is at the midpoint of the Gemini navamsha, its *basic* contribution is two and one-half years. As such, the most duration the basic (or first) dasha can contribute to life is twelve years; this would be at the end of the Pisces navamsha.

Now (potentially) there are deductions. There cannot be more than one deduction per planet. Reductions precede increases in amsayu. If there is more than one deduction possible, then only the highest deduction is calculated. After the basic duration has been calculated, there will often be either a reduction or an increase or both.

If a chart has planets in houses seven through twelve, if a planet is above the horizon in the chart, a deduction is usually going to apply to each of them. A malefic in the twelfth loses its full duration; in the 11th, half; in the 10th, one-third; in the 9th, one-fourth; in the 8th, one-fifth; in the seventh, one-sixth. Benefics also takes losses when above the horizon, but not as great: In the twelfth, one-half; in the 11th, one-fourth; in the 10th, one-sixth; in the 9th, one-eighth; in the eighth, one-tenth; in the seventh, one-twelfth.

When there is more than one planet in any of these houses, only the most powerful planet amongst the group takes his scheduled loss.

After this calculation is made for planets eligible to receive it, if the reduction is less than one-third, there may be an alternative reduction that is applied. If a planet is in its enemy's sign, it loses one-third of its basic duration, except when it is retrograde. If it was already reduced by being in the seventh through twelfth houses, the planet does not get reduced for a second time—unless that first reduction was less than one-third; only the reduction of greatest amount (of two or more potential reductions) is applied. If a planet is combust, it loses one-half of its duration; this rule, however, does not apply to Venus or Saturn for some reason.

Calculation of the lagna dasha has its own special rules. If the lagna is strong, then it grants as many years as it is situated from Aries in the natal chart. Proportional subdivisions of lagna itself must be included in this calculation. For example, a lagna in the middle of Sagittarius would grant eight and one-half years of dasha length. If the lagna is not strong, then the number of years of its dasha is determined differently: It is determined by the number of navamshas (of that sign) that have risen above the horizon at birth, but another opinion says that it is the number of navamshas from the most recent Aries in the series.

In the pindayu and nisargayu systems, there are no increases of the length of the dasha; those dashas are calculated in terms of how close the planet is to either exaltation or debilitation. In the amshayu, there are increases.

The planets have sometimes already been modified by a reduction; this is the figure that is used to make calculations of increases (not the basic calculation) in amshayu. The years to be increased will either be from the basic duration (if there were no deductions) or to the *adjusted* dasha. There can also not be more than one increase to a planet's duration of dasha. The highest increase attains when there is more than one possible.

If a planet is exalted, multiply its basic or adjusted duration by three. Do the same if it is retrograde. In its own or exalted navamsha, multiply the basic or adjusted duration times two. Also do the same when it is found to be vargottama or even in its own dreshkana. Swami Vijnananda adds:

"The whole period of life . . . is actually seen in cases where the individual lives according to shastric rules and rites. But if the individual lives an immoral, unclean life, this period gets diminished."

The converse similarly applies: If you live a very elevated or transcendental lifestyle, your duration of life may be extended by the Kala Purusha and even the Cosmic Maintainer, Lord Vishnu.

I have given you only the basics in this chapter. Obviously, in order to calculate your length of life, and the length of the dashas comprising it, you would need more knowledge in a similarly organized format. At octave two, it is counterproductive to provide this, as mistakes will almost invariably be made. The comprehensive instructional course gets fully into it, however, and there we shall take you to the third octave of the sidereal science. At that level, you will understand the calculation of the dashas.

Knowing what is scheduled to be your termination point is often hard to handle. I do calculate basic natal charts for individuals, separate from the instructional course (consult Appendix One for more details on the services). If someone approaches me to explain their chart, I cannot make sure that they also become qualified as an experienced astrologer, obviously. Only in the detailed natal chart, the second level natal chart, do I provide the dashas. Although only preliminaries of the dasha methods have been expounded in this chapter, it is can still be a bit overwhelming in its details. However, once you get the system (or, you could say, three systems) down, it is not extremely difficult to comprehend and apply; it is meticulous.

Also, according to Brihat Parashara Hora, very short life is known as Bala Rishta. It is described in that work as being of a duration of up to eight years. Varahamihira has dedicated a complete chapter to it early in his book. Every combination he describes for bala-rishta in that chapter indicates death either right after birth or sometime in the first year.

Next, we come to Mrityu Yoga, although my <u>Brihat Parashara Hora</u> translation calls it Yoga Rishta. It runs from age eight through twenty. After this, we have three divisions of life spans: Short, medium, and long. Short duration runs up to the age of thirty-six (some say up to thirty-two and others say up to forty years of age). Medium lifespan is said in the <u>Brihat Parashara Hora</u> to run up to the age of sixty-four; elsewhere the figure of seventy-two years is described to be its high end. From one of these maximums (of medium life), long life span is said to be of a length of up to one-hundred and twenty years.

There are rectifications listed in the <u>Brihat Parashara Hora</u>; these are supposed to extend the astrological calculations for a short life or a medium life or even a somewhat long life. Good yogas increase the life span, and these rectifications are all good yogas.

For example, if a kendra contains a benefic and the lord of lagna is conjunct that benefic, or receives a full aspect from a benefic (in particular, benefic Jupiter), then this rectification is supposed to produce a longer duration of life. If the lord of lagna is in a quadrant conjunct with, or receiving a full aspect from, benefic Jupiter and Venus, a longer duration of life is indicated. If the lord of lagna is conjunct an exalted planet, longer life, or an extension of long life, is indicated. If the lord of the ascendant is in a quadrant and is stronger than the lord of the eighth, then a similar long-life rectification yoga is produced (automatic for a Libra lagna). There are, in the <u>Brihat Parashara Hora</u>, no less than fifteen of these life extension yogas listed.

Length of life is a very complex topic, and you need the direct mercy of *Source* localized in order to know what is going to be your exact duration of life. In some very special cases, He can extend life past what was karmically scheduled according to material destiny.

There is another interesting short-cut method given in <u>BHP</u>. Most sidereal astrologers are aware of this method, and they combine it with vimshottari. I call this method the Triplicate Set of Determiners. It consists of three sets of combinations, and each of these sets is comprised of two components. As aforementioned, the signs are divided into moveable signs, fixed signs, and dual signs, and these figure into this triplicate.

In the first set, you look to the sign of the location of the lagna lord and the sign of the location of the lord of the eighth house; for a Libra ascendant, this will be the same sign. In the second set of determiners, you look to the sign of the location of Saturn and the sign of the location of the Moon. In the third set, the most important one, you look to the sign of the lord of lagna and the sign of the lord of the hour.

Concerning this last calculation (of the third set), the daylight duration and the nighttime duration are divided into hours. These are also known as horas (from which we have derived the term "hours"). These horas are different from the two horas that subdivide every sign, although there is a related equivalency to them. Every decent astrological program will calculate the lord of the hour of your birth; these hours are not exactly the same as our fixed sixty minutes of clock time. The lord of the hour of your birth is located in a sign; that sign is either moveable, fixed, or dual. We are looking at all six positions comprising these three sets of determiners.

If all three sets have both components moveable, then that indicates 120 years of life. If two of the sets have both components moveable, that indicates 108 years of life. If all three sets have one component fixed and the other dual, then that indicates 120 years of life. If two of the three sets have one component fixed and the other dual, then that similarly indicates 108 years of life. There is more to it than this, obviously.

In concluding this important chapter, I should like to point out that, if you accept vimshottari rather than the pindayu method, the nisargayu method of dashas (if Moon is the strongest), or the am-shayu method, then you are not going to actually know your dashas. If you happen to know what dasha you are in through vimshottari, that is accidental. After all, a stopped clock is still accurate twice a day. We should not rely on the Law of Accident.

Instead, if we undergo the painstaking task of calculating and ascertaining our dashas (life stages) according to one of the above-mentioned three methods, we shall see the correlation—in terms of dashas that have passed.

That will be most valuable, because then we can know how to predict the current dasha and the one after that. This allows us to chart a course through knowledge. We become more successful also. As Clint Eastwood said: "A man has to know his limitations." If you know your current and approaching dashas, you will know your limitations.

If they are very good ones, you can plan to put the petal to the metal and go full out to achieve your ambitions. If and/or when these ambitions are fixed in buddhi-yoga, so much the better for you.

Chapter Nine

ON OCCUPATION

The acquisition of wealth is often linked to occupation, so this chapter will be given priority by many of my readers. There are two major rules for determining occupation. By occupation, we mean that kind of avocation that suits an individual astrologically. The topic is somewhat intricate and voluminous, but it is still quite comprehensible.

There are two chief rules. When the first rule obtains, then the second rule becomes irrelevant. When the first rule does not obtain, the second rule comes into force by default.

First, look to see if any of the seven major planets is in either the tenth house from the ascendant or the tenth house from the Moon. The tenth house is the house of success as well as occupation. A planet's presence in one of these two houses activates the first rule. A planet present (or planets present) in one or both of these houses indicates the kind of occupation which best leads to a lucrative, satisfying, and successful career.

Let me now explain Rule One. For example, you would have to look to a planet being in the second house if the Moon was in the fifth. Remember to check out both of the abovementioned tenths (not just from lagna) when analyzing your chart in terms of occupational synchronicity.

A planet in one of these houses will certainly bestow wealth (through that indicated occupation) during its dasha or antardasha. Nevertheless, these influences will always be there as a part of your general life process. More than one planet may be activated according to Rule One. That must be considered good karma, because it means that multiple lines of work will be suitable for you to make a reasonable livelihood.

Every occupation, without exception, has a specific planet that governs it in this material world. For example, an auto mechanic would be governed by Saturn, as per avocation. A medical man would be governed by the Sun, and Mars would govern a sportsman. A courier would be governed by Mercury, and all nautical employment would be governed by Moon. An actor would be governed by

Venus, and a professor would be governed by Jupiter. I have simply given here a small listing of occupations.

More knowledge is required if you're interested in other professions or occupational lines. Neglecting this study could lead to choosing a wrong field; that's bad karma. Selecting an occupation that you are not astrologically suited for is an invitation for all kinds of setbacks, obstacles, and disillusionments in ordinary life.

From my experience, it is better to have at least one planet in the tenth from lagna or the Moon than to not have such a planet in one of those houses. When one or both of those houses are occupied, avocation tends to proceed easily. Obviously, a malefic in the tenth will generally hurt the house, but it will nevertheless indicate how you can make a living.

Now, often no planet or planets will be found in the tenth from lagna or the Moon. That activates Rule Two. That rule generally—at least, more often than not—makes three planets the determiners of avocation. To find these planets (in some infrequent cases, it will be only one planet), we look to the Sun, the Moon, and the lagna. Then we look to the signs of the tenth houses from the Sun, the Moon, and the ascendant.

This is going to get a little complicated, so remain attentive. I considered this chapter to be just barely eligible for inclusion in the teaching of Sidereal Science/Octave Two. However, it is too important to leave it to the instructional course alone; some of you are not scheduled to follow up.

We determine the lords of the signs of the tenth houses from the Sun, the Moon, and the ascendant (in some cases, it will only be one lord). If the Sun and the Moon were conjunct in the ascendant, that would be an example of only one such lord. You can use your intelligence to figure out some of the other ways, especially if one of those applies to you.

Now, look to see in which navamshas these three planets (or two or one) are situated. This is getting closer to the final step of this Rule Two process. Each of those navamshas will have a lord. We have discussed the lords of the navamsha vargas many times, and you can consult the table of navamsha lords to advantage in Appendix Two. The final step is to correlate this lord of the navamsha with the avocation, because he determines it. In other words, that navamsha lord indicates occupational synchronicity.

Even without planets in the tenth from lagna or the Moon, Rule Two, when thus activated, will always yield at least one such navamsha lord. More often than that, at least two of them will be activated; even more often than that, three such separate navamsha lords determine avocation.

Let us return to Rule One. If the planet in the tenth house from the ascendant or the Moon is the Sun, a person's father facilitates avocation. If it be the Moon, then the mother is the facilitator. If it be Mars, then enemies help you prosper in your avocation. If it be Mercury, friends are the facilitators. If it be Jupiter, then brothers facilitate your occupational development. If it be Saturn, then servants generally help you.

No such facilitators are mentioned in connection to Rule Two; this is one of the chief reasons why it is better to have Rule One active in your chart. The facilitation will be most prominent during the dasha or antardasha of that planet, as aforementioned.

Proceeding again to Rule Two, if the Sun is lord of the navamsha (determined by the step-by-step procedures detailed above) be the Sun, then a person earns through occupations connected to scents, gold, wool, and medicines. Obviously, Rule One and Rule Two have a correlation in these descriptions. When the Moon rules the navamsha, then a person earns through occupations connected to agriculture, articles from seas or rivers, from women, from one's mother, and from security occupations. When it is Mars, he earns through occupations connected to war, weapons, sports, cooking, fire, machinery (particularly driving or operating them), metals, as well various heroic activities.

When it is Mercury, he earns through occupations connected to reading, math, writing, poetry, and mechanical drawing. In actuality, there are many occupations governed by Mercury. When it is Jupiter, he earns as a teacher, a professor, through ecclesiastical connections, from affiliations with learned men, from worship of Deities, and from pilgrimages. Although BJ did not list it, when the navamsha lord is Jupiter, banking is also indicated. Jupiter being this navamsha lord also facilitates earning through charities, mining, minerals, as well as austerity.

If Venus is the ruler of the navamsha, he earns through occupations connected to gemstones, queens (both kinds), sales, jewelry, silver, entertainment, as well as horses and buffalo (horseracing, however, would be governed by Mars). If Saturn is the lord of the navamsha, he earns things the hard way, through low and even criminal acts, sometimes unsuitable to his rank and station. He can earn through acts of torture or killing, e.g., slaughterhouses, or through some avocations connected to machines (as per industrial enterprises). He can be a prison guard or an executioner as well. Unless there are counter-indicators, if Saturn is the navamsha lord, hard work is a person's lot in occupational life.

Rule Two must be understood in even further detail. Look to the ruler of the navamsha where the lord of the tenth from Sun, Moon, or lagna is situated. The lord of the tenth from Sun, Moon, or lagna has a planetary relationship with that lord of that particular navamsha. If that lord of the navamsha is his friend, then a person taking up the indicated occupation will find that wealth is secured from, or in relation with, his friends.

If that navamsha lord is an enemy to the lord of the tenth from the Sun, Moon, or lagna, then the indicated avocation will dictate that earnings come from enemies or competitors.

If that navamsha lord be the same planet, then wealth in that avocation is connected to one's own inner circle. The inner circle could be the family, a club, a group (like a rock group), a social network, or a cult.

When the lord of the navamsha is himself in exaltation in the chart and is also bright and powerful, then one obtains wealth from virtually any avocation; he does so on the basis of his own prowess. In other words, he is good at being a Jack-of-all-Trades.

These calculations can be a little tedious, but ultimately they are not complicated to the point of futility—once you get the system down.

Here are some last notes in connection to this chapter. Although it is about avocation or occupation, there are separate planetary placements connected to obtaining wealth. Varahamihira elected to mention them in his chapter on the topic of livelihood. When there are powerful benefics in the ascendant, the second, and/or the eleventh, a person secures wealth easily from the avocation of his choice. That makes occupational selection easier.

Positive yogas between the lord of the second and the lord of the eleventh, or between the lord of the first and either of those two lords, make endeavors to obtain wealth proceed downstream. An exalted planet in the ascendant or in the second, as lord of the second or the eleventh, would also activate this good karma, as far as wealth is concerned.

When obtaining wealth becomes more or less a non-issue, avocation can be researched in terms of interest and preference. I was originally attracted to study this science in order to figure out what line of work I was suited for astrologically. I did not get the revelation until later in my studies; as discussed previously, it took me some time to ascertain the correct ayanamsha. According to the Lahiri ayanamsha (and most of the others), my Venus would be exalted in navamsha; there was absolutely no historical vindication of this conclusion. On the other hand, if Venus (one of the planets involved in determining my avocation) was placed in the navamsha of Mars, it activated a reading there that made complete sense—and there was plenty of history to back it up. Although I have five benefic yogas in one of my houses (obviously, a quadrant), my astrological occupations are only very indirectly indicated by that house.

Utility is the principle. A description of how to determine your best occupations is now within reach. Occult knowledge and realization is not limited to utopian or internal speculations; it can also have utilitarian or pragmatic value. In terms of the chart, occupational options, when analyzed and understood, offer an opportunity to reveal your path to wealth and success.

Chapter Ten

ELECTION PRINCIPLES

In order to take advantage of election benefits at the higher level of the third octave, you have to receive the knowledge, be competent enough to understand its general principles, and be skilled, diligent, and meticulous enough to apply it. Having a good muhurtha module in your computer is helpful, and having a very good memory is even more helpful. You must have paid the price before you can do any of this. You have purchased this sidereal primer, so to that extent you have paid the price; you should become qualified to be an astrologer at the second octave or level. An occultist has to apply himself to all the facets and angles of election astrology; it can be frustrating (at times) and is an ocean of details.

Sometimes, a day will not at all lend itself to auspicious elections; this can even be the case for a week or more (although, this is usually not so). For example, if Mercury is combust and Jupiter is the only unblemished benefic, putting him in the ascendant may not solve the problems. If he is turned into a malefic for that ascendant, you should not place him there. If putting him in the ascendant also puts Mars in the eighth, you should not accept that chart. Some would argue that, if Mars is exalted in the eighth in such an election chart, you could make an exception. That's a razor's edge call. Still, all sidereal astrologers would agree that, for most of the lagnas, you do not want Mars in the eighth in any election chart.

If malefic Saturn is with Mars in lagna, simply putting Sun or Moon in the eleventh would not, in my view, be enough to overcome such an afflicted ascendant. There are many negative planetary arrangements that present all kinds of dilemmas. As Raman so aptly put it, a human being is daily assaulted by a stupendous number of negative influences.

We are not going to delineate, in this primer, all of the categories of initiatives that can be elected. Nor, obviously, are we going to detail all the planetary placements that specifically favor those particular initiatives. Instead, in this chapter, we are going to present an overview of election astrology at the level of two octave. That should not be misunderstood to mean that there will be no details here; there will plenty. We shall describe some benefic mitigation possibilities, as well as the malefic juxtapositions that should best be avoided.

Becoming a competent sidereal astrologer takes time and effort. Until that ability has been attained, it is recommended to seek out assistance for this determination (election astrology) from a person who can provide it. After assimilating this chapter, your election competency will be at octave two. For some relatively inconsequential elections, you can apply the principles you have herein learned and see how it all plays out; on average, things should meet your level of expectation. For very important elections, however, you should consult an astrologer who is at a higher level (such as octave three) and let him or her do the work. Alternatively, you can take the instructional curriculum and become a C.O.R.E. sidereal astrologer yourself. Election astrology is emphasized in that course.

An election chart must always be correlated with the natal chart. In particular, the natal placement of the Moon must be considered. One of the reasons for this is that there is a cycle of the Moon that repeats on a regular basis. The janma-nakshatra is the birth constellation of the Moon; a person often feels weak or gets a little sick when the Moon transits this lunar mansion. The nakshatra that follows it is favorable and conducive to wealth during the Moon's transit through it. The one after that is unfavorable and conducive to some kind of loss or expense.

The fourth nakshatra of this cycle, during lunar transit, is again favorable and produces gains. The fifth one is stressful; it provides a test in the form of obstacles. The sixth one is the best of the cycle, and it is known as realized ambitions. The seventh transit of the Moon is the worst; it is often dangerous, especially in the first paryaya (that will be detailed subsequently in this chapter). The eighth transit provides relief, and it is good. The ninth transit is even better; it is very good.

Then the Moon returns to a constellation that corresponds with its janma-nakshatra. The nine-nakshatra cycle starts again, with this constellation also indicating weakness or ill health. The cycle of nine keeps continually repeating, and, since there are twenty-seven of these lunar mansions in the zodiac, there are consequently three of these sets of cycles per revolution of the Moon through the signs.

Fixing auspicious election times depends upon this nakshatra cycle. The chart should best have a favorable relationship to the natal chart. Even a very good election chart (objectively) is prone to produce bad effects, at least to some degree, if the initiative is strongly counter-indicated by the birth chart. Sometimes, an excellent election chart decreases the chances of complete failure, even when the initiative is counter-indicated by the natal chart—but only when the afflictions in the birth chart aren't overwhelming. Some election combinations are so powerful that they can overcome all but the most afflicted indicators in the janma-kundali.

At the same time, it is a virtual certainty that there will be some kind of blemish or blemishes found in any election chart. I have calculated hundreds of these in the course of my astrological career. During that time, only once could I say that I came up with an election chart in which *every* planet was favorably situated. The easy results I obtained after moving into that apartment in Houston on that lagna were fantastic.

There are five considerations that automatically enter into the determination of an auspicious time for an election. These are: 1) the nakshatra of the Moon, 2) the lunar phase, also known as the tithi or lunar day, 3) the day of the week, 4) the yoga that is operative at that time, and 5) the karana. I do pay some attention to the yoga, in the sense that I try to avoid the five negative ones. I do not consider the karana at all; if it is negative, it can be overcome by other factors quite easily.

Of these five, the nakshatra, the tithi, and the weekday should always be considered for any election chart. These three, along with lagna, factor into an important calculation. Pay attention to this *computation*, which will be described in this chapter. We have discussed the nakshatras already, and we have described them in some detail; their order was presented. Each nakshatra consists of thirteen degrees and twenty minutes.

So, let us now consider the tithi or lunar phase. There are thirty different tithies in a lunar month; this is one perspective. Another viewpoint is that there are only sixteen tithies. Here's how to understand this apparent contradiction. The lunar month is divided into two halves: The waxing Moon and the waning Moon. The waxing Moon peaks on the full Moon night, which is known as purnima. Then the Moon begins to wane, reaching the termination of that half cycle on the new Moon day, which is known as amavasya. Each of the moon phases in these halves shares the same numbers—with only one exception. They both share the numbers from one to fourteen in the cycle, e.g., the first day after the new Moon is called first day wax (with the number one), and the first day after the full Moon is called first day wane (also with the number one). The new Moon (amavasya), however, is given the number thirty, while the full Moon (purnima) is given the number fifteen. These numbers play an essential role in the *computation*.

Some of these tithies are auspicious and some are not helpful for the majority of election charts. Most of the inauspicious ones can still be worked with as long as other factors are strong and benefic. Each tithi consists of twelve degrees of sidereal arc. These degrees are calculated as per an interrelationship between the Sun and the Moon. For example, if the Moon is twenty-four degrees ahead of the Sun, that would mean that it is just entering the *third* tithi wax; its number for the computation would obviously be *three*. You can calculate all the other phases accordingly.

The eleventh tithi of both the waxing and waning Moon is excellent for fasting, particularly from grains, beans, and legumes. The fourth tithi, the sixth tithi, the eighth tithi, and the twelfth tithi are considered generally inauspicious in both their waxing and waning halves. The twelfth tithi is generally not bad if fasting was observed on the eleventh tithi.

However, there are some tithies that are really dreadful; the worst one is the fourteenth tithi wane. This fourteenth tithi is quite inauspicious during the waxing phase, but it is terribly so during the waning Moon cycle. And the tithi which follows it, the new Moon tithi (amavasya), is also very negative. I do not attempt activities (in terms of calculating an election chart) during these two lunar phases; I have only made one exception to this. Some are of the opinion that the full Moon night is also inauspicious; I do not share that view whatsoever.

The full Moon has significantly heightened energy to be sure. It can be wild. Nevertheless, I will use it for almost all election considerations. There is an occult principle connected to the full Moon: Things tend to culminate or fructify on the full Moon and new Moon days. Indeed, there is a cycle of five related to this. Every fifth tithi—on the fifth tithi, the tenth tithi, and the full Moon or new Moon—there is often some kind of fructification or culmination. There is a negative period connected to the tithies at these fructification points; it is connected specifically to *their endings* or termination junctures. That is called tithi gandanthara.

Concerning the weekday, it is a very straightforward and simple calculation. During the reformation of the calendar, i.e., when the Gregorian calendar replaced the Julian, we can thank our lucky stars (pun intended) that the weekday was not also changed—or that it was not "re-adjusted." The days have their lords, and it is not a difficult pattern to assimilate: Sun-day; Moon-day; Tiu's-day (Tiu was the Norse god of war, Mars); Woden's-day (Mercury); Thor's-day (Jupiter); Frau's-day (Venus), and Saturn's-day. In the subsequent *computation* formula—the one that employs the nakshatra, the tithi, the weekday, and the lagna—each day is numbered as per its chronological listing. Sun is given the number one, Moon is given two . . . Saturn is given the number seven. You would prefer that the lord of the day be strong in an election chart.

Regarding the yoga, basically I only consider it in terms of the five negative ones. The yoga is calculated via another Sun-Moon interrelationship; that formula is a bit more complicated than the one for the tithi. Any decent sidereal program will list the yoga operative at the time you are considering. The yogas to be avoided are: Atiganda, shula, ganda, vaidhriti, and vyatipat. This last-mentioned yoga is very malefic. The negative yogas only have their malefic effects before the middle of the day (midpoint between sunrise and sunset, also called abhijit); after that, they are powerless—this is important to remember.

There are twenty-seven yogas. Aside from the abovementioned five, the other twenty-two are either acceptable or favorable. There are also highly auspicious days known as siddha-yogas. When these occur, the siddha-yoga replaces the otherwise scheduled yoga. Siddha-yogas are most excellent for all auspicious endeavors.

In an election chart, the Moon should be made both strong and favorable. If you have to accept a mediocre Moon for some reason, make sure the other factors or indicators are as propitious as possible. Another essential calculation is the strength of lagna. We could certainly say that lagna is the most important consideration in any election chart. You want both lagna and the lord of lagna strong in the chart. Different initiatives sometimes require variations, i.e., different houses are fortified, inasmuch as those houses are directly connected to the election initiative. Still, lagna must always be given priority; the next priority is Moon.

Every lagna has a certain portion that is to be rejected—even in an excellent ascendant. This part is called the lagna-tyaga. On Monday and Friday, this lagna-tyaga is the last navamsha of the signs

Cancer, Scorpio, Capricorn, and Pisces. On Wednesdays and Saturdays, the first navamshas of Aries, Taurus, Virgo, and Sagittarius constitute the lagna-tyaga. On Tuesday, Thursdays, and Sundays, the fifth navamsha of Gemini, Leo, Libra, and Aquarius must be rejected. Actually, I take it a step farther, i.e., I avoid the lagna-tyaga as per the weekdays specified and do not limit that application simply to specific lagnas on certain weekdays.

Concerning the weekdays, Tuesday morning is to be rejected unless a siddha-yoga is active (or Sun in the eleventh, or other mitigating factors). The whole of Saturday is not very good for election activities, but if Saturn is exalted or in its own signs, then it is very good. All days are made good when their lords are strong and well-placed in the zodiac. All days can also be made good if the quadrants are fortified with benefics, as well.

Just as each of the twelve lagnas had a lagna-tyaga period, similarly, each nakshatra (of the Moon) has a negative period that lasts for about one and one half hours. This period is very difficult to calculate; figuring it is cumbersome work. As long as you get a favorable navamsha ascendant, this stricture can be neglected. The Moon does not move through the nakshatras at the same speed at any given time. If the sidereal software you use makes this calculation (of nakshatra-tyaga), great. Otherwise, strengthen whatever you can and don't be overly concerned about it.

Let us now look at the big picture: Overall principles. If Jupiter is neither combust or debilitated—and he is not a malefic for that ascendant—placing him in lagna can overcome a host of obstacles or inauspicious planetary juxtapositions (incidentally, and as a reminder, another name for a planetary juxtaposition is yoga). Placing benefic Mercury in the ascendant (under the same restrictions as abovementioned) accomplishes almost the same thing. You don't want a malefic in the ascendant, and you do not want Mercury conjunct a malefic (because then he *usually* becomes one). Benefic Venus in the ascendant is not quite as powerful there as benefic Jupiter and benefic Mercury, but he can still serve to overcome most of the bad influences in an election chart. Make sure that your election lagna, in those cases, is a favorable sign as far as Venus is concerned. Placing *any* exalted planet in the ascendant will overcome a host of evils, and this will also be the case if an exalted planet is placed in any of the quadrants in an election chart.

Making the lord of lagna strong is also very important. You do not want him in the sixth, eighth, or twelfth houses. Placing the lord of lagna in a quadrant or a trine is the best. If he is also closely conjunct an exalted planet, all the better—of course, you don't always have an exalted planet to work with in a given timeframe. Placing the lord of lagna in the ascendant is always a good fortification.

If at all possible, select a day wherein the lord of that weekday is either exalted, in his own house, conjunct a benefic, or dignified. If you cannot achieve this, make sure that other factors compensate for it.

The Sun and the Moon are most excellent in the eleventh, removing many negative influences from the election chart. Of course, the Moon should not be combust or in debilitation. Some are of the opinion that Moon in the eleventh during the day does not serve to mitigate inauspiciousness in the chart; I do not concur with them, however.

Here is something interesting. If both the Sun and the Moon *are together* in the eleventh (which can only happen sometime in the late morning, of course), that will almost always be propitious *as far as the Sun is concerned*. It becomes (using Orwellian language here) double-plus good only if the Moon is not combust. This is the case when Moon is either in the second tithi wax (near the end of the sign) or in the thirteenth tithi wane (near the beginning of the sign). I would not consider Sun and Moon in the eleventh propitious if Moon is in the fourteenth tithi wane.

The more you can place benefics in the quadrants in your election chart, the better it will be. The more you can place the malefics in the eleventh, the stronger the chart will work for you. When you can't get a malefic in the eleventh, see if you can get the malefics in the third and/or sixth houses. Some would say that plugging a malefic in the twelfth also works; that's another razor's edge call; I'm ambivalent about it.

The Moon's janma nakshatra is supposed to have a favorable relation to the election chart. We have already explained the three sets of nine repeating nakshatras. Besides the janma nakshatra, the Moon was also in a specific sign in the natal chart; this is called its janma rashi. In the election chart, you do not want to place the Moon in a sign that happens to be the sixth, eight, or twelfth from your janma rashi. You can ignore this stricture if certain other mitigations are active in the election chart. If the Moon and the lord of the eighth are friends, that is one such nullification. If the Moon is waxing, exalted, in a favorable sign, in a favorable navamsha, and/or is strong, that is an even greater mitigation.

Now, we must apply these principles to the *computation*. It is a relatively simple mathematical calculation. It is called the panchaka, and pancha means five. There are five components to this formula; one of them is procedural (process). First, we must consider the nakshatra of the Moon and what number is to be assigned to it. If it is in its janma nakshatra, then it would receive a number one in value. If it is in the nakshatra just previous to the janma nakshatra, it would receive a number twenty-seven. You should be able to understand the principle of how to attain this number for the lunar nakshatra of the election chart from these two examples.

That was the first component; now let us proceed to the second one. This simply involves the number of the tithi; it does not matter whether it is waxing or waning. Remember, full Moon is fifteen, and the number for the new Moon is thirty (but you won't undertake elections on amavasya).

The third component is lagna. Aries equals one, Taurus equals two . . . Pisces equals twelve; the principle here is obvious.

The fourth component is the weekday: Sunday receives a number one, Monday receives a number two . . . Saturday receives a number seven. You add all of these four values together. Their sum is then divided by nine (this addition and division is the procedural component).

We are only concerned about the remainder. If nine divides evenly, then the remainder is zero. That is a good indicator, i.e., the election chart is favorable. The other favorable remainders are three, five, and seven. The unfavorable remainders, obviously, are 1,2,4,6, and 8.

Nevertheless, there are mitigations to be considered even if an unfavorable remainder is obtained. On the whole, it's best to discard a panchaka that is unfavorable. However, if there are many strong positions and benefic placements in the election chart, then you can accept it (despite a negative panchaka) only if the following negatives are not present: If the election concerns employment or occupation, do not accept a panchaka where the remainder is four. If the election concerns house construction, do not lay the foundation if the remainder after division of the sum is either two or four. If the election concerns travel, do not accept it if the remainder is six. If the election is about the marriage ceremony, do not accept the lagna that produces a re-mainder of one or eight in the panchaka computation.

Returning to the aforementioned cycle of three sets of nine nak-shatras: Each of these sets is called a paryaya. This is important, espe-cially in relation to the negative nakshatras. Again, those are the first, the third, the fifth, and especially the seventh in the series. You gener-ally want to avoid them in election charts. However, the power of these transits of the Moon to cause harm diminishes as each paryaya advances.

In other words, on your janma nakshatra lunar transit, feeling weak or even sick will be most pronounced; this is because it com-mences the first paryaya. The first paryaya shows the effects of the nine nakshatra transits very powerfully. In that paryaya, the seventh nakshatra will be most dangerous and fully operative.

After you pass through the first set of nine (the first paryaya), you enter the second paryaya, commencing with the tenth nakshatra from your janma nakshatra. Here the constellational transits are not as intense. They are operative, but you can overcome the negative ones more easily.

The third paryaya commences with the nineteenth constellation from your janma nakshatra. Here the nakshatras only have a shadow effect, and it is almost negligible. This does not mean that I recom-mend utilizing the beginning of a danger nakshatra in this paryaya for your election.

This principle in relation to the paryayas applies to both posi-tive lunar transits through the nakshatras, as well as to negative ones. However, even in the first paryaya, the evil influences of a negative transit do not hold sway for the whole duration of that transit. In the first paryaya, the evil of the first transit (weakness or sickness of the body) only lasts for about the first three and one-half hours. The evil of the third transit (loss) lasts only for about two hours. The evil of the fifth transit (obstacles) lasts only about four hours. The evil of the worst transit, the seventh (danger) lasts for about the first three hours. Obviously, things improve in relation to this principle in the second paryaya, due to its lessened intensity.

Select a software program with a good sidereal election or mu-hurtha feature. See if it calculates the aforementioned siddha-yogas. I am not going to list all of the seventy-three different combinations that produce these special yogas. Sixty-six of them are determined via a threefold combination of day, nakshatra, and tithi. The other six are simpler: Sunday corresponding with Hasta; Monday corresponding with Shravana; Tuesday with Ashvini; Wednesday coinciding with Anuradha; Thursday with Pushya; Friday with Revati; Saturday corresponding with Rohini.

A siddha-yoga may be operative at sunrise, but, later in the day, the tithi or nakshatra switches; that ends the siddha-yoga. Similarly, a siddha-yoga may be not be operative at sunrise, but later in the day or night, due to the emergence of a new tithi or nakshatra, a siddha-yoga emerges.

There are specific evils to be avoided in an election chart. There are some factors that can neutralize or mitigate many of them in most cases. Still, when these great evils are present, it's best to not accept that timeframe for your election. The first one is called Surya sankramana. The Sun enters into a new sign somewhere in the middle of the month. The moment of its actual entrance is accurately determined only with an accurate ayanamsha; I have provided you that. Six and one-half hours before this transit, as well as six and one-half hours after it, are jinxed.

Never allow two malefics to hem in the lagna from their placements in the second and twelfth houses. Never allow two malefics to hem in a benefic in a quadrant, i.e., all three planets being in the same sign and house.

The Moon should best not be associated with a malefic.

Now we come to muhurtha. Sometimes, election astrology is called muhurtha. Calculation of the muhurtha is cumbersome; this is because its duration varies. It is a small division of time that applies to the lagna or point of the ascendant. There are thirty muhurthas: Fifteen during daylight and fifteen at night. During the equinox, all these muhurthas have the same duration, obviously. This duration changes radically during days in and around the solstice times.

If you want to personally calculate the muhurthas for the day or the night, you need to know the time of sunrise and sunset on the given date in a given place. On Sunday, the negative muhurthas during the day are the first, second, fourth, tenth, eleventh, twelfth, fourteenth, and fifteenth. The negative muhurthas during Sunday at night are the first, second, sixth, and seventh. It can get complicated without a good software program.

Using numbers now, let us simplify the **generic** bad muhurthas for all seven days of the week: During the day: 1,2,4,10,11,12,15. During the night: 1,2,6,7. In other words, on Sunday, the fourteenth diurnal muhurtha is added to this generic list. On Monday, the eighth diurnal muhurtha is added. On Thursday, the thirteenth diurnal muhurtha is added. And on Friday, the eighth diurnal muhurtha also becomes negative.

Simply do your research and select a sidereal software program that includes automatic calculation of the muhurtha, as well as its status, i.e., whether it is positive or negative. The selection of a good muhurtha—also sometimes known as "a moment"—should not be neglected. It is certainly more important than the lord of the hour. Analyzing the muhurtha possibilities entails fine-tuning your election chart. Simply keep trying different times in the favorable lagna until you come up with a positive muhurtha (sometimes it is not possible, but not that often). If the chart is outstanding—but you can only secure a negative muhurtha—let the chart overcome it, i.e., accept that election time and don't lose the great lagna.

Besides the muhurtha, there is a similar (ultimately unrelated) consideration in relation to the ascendant *of the navamsha chart*. If your software includes this feature, then it is very good software. You do not want a malefic in the navamsha ascendant; fine-tuning again comes into play here, as it did with locating a muhurtha in a favorable election lagna.

Then there is the negative factor called gandanthara, which we have briefly mentioned already in both of its two facets. I once got victimized big-time by tithi-gandanthara, so I learned the hard way never to accept an election chart under its malignant influence. It is a very great evil. It is based on lunar transits between either signs or tithies.

When the Moon is transiting from a water sign to a fire sign, that is sign-gandanthara; when it is transiting from a culmination tithi to another tithi (we have mentioned these fructification tithies previously in this chapter), it is tithi-gandanthara. In the rare event when these two gandantharas coincide, look out! That will be a very ominous span.

The three hours (total time) before and after the Moon transits from Cancer to Leo, from Scorpio to Sagittarius, and from Pisces to Aries is called sign-gandanthara. The three hours (total time) before and after the Moon transits from the fifth tithi to the sixth tithi, from the tenth tithi to the eleventh tithi, and from the fifteenth or thirtieth tithi to the first tithi is known as tithi-gandanthara. Gandanthara applies to both lunar phases.

The next evil is difficult to calculate. The reason for this is that I do not know of any current sidereal program that *accurately* calculates shad-bala. You do not want malefics stronger in the election chart than the benefics. Study the chapter I have provided on this topic in order to make a rough determination for your potential election chart. Remember that a malefic is no longer so when it is exalted.

The next great evil is Mars in the eighth. As such, there is always one ascendant every day (or night) that should be discarded.

The next evil is Venus in the sixth. If Venus were exalted or in Mula Trikona in the sixth—and if there were outstanding factors as well that nullify evils—I would accept Venus in the sixth.

The next negative conjunction: Do not let the election lagna be the sign ruling the eighth house from your natal ascendant. This is a tough one, because sometimes that lagna may be outstanding. It's a personal call.

When both the Sun and the Moon are moving in the same direction and are at the same declination point, it is an inauspicious time. Some opine that it is inauspicious even if they are connected in this way while moving in opposite directions—and I agree with that.

Finally, we come to the topic of omens (often a result of curses). For example, the nakshatra in which either a solar or lunar eclipse has occurred is jinxed for six months after the occurrence. You do not want to perform the marriage ceremony, in particular, when the Moon is there. Always be aware of obvious negative omens at the commencement of any initiative (or just before it). Give up that time and start again with your calculations; in your calculations, something was overlooked.

Let me point out some other subtleties from direct experience. Do not allow anyone—particularly an inimical person—to be intimately involved in your initiative, conscious that you have calculated it astrologically. This applies to mundaners: Atheists, demoniac persons, and non-occultists in general. Let me assure you that they will go out of their way to mess you up. Not only will you not wind up with a good result, the initiative will most definitely yield only bad results. Do not neglect this warning.

At first glance, it would appear that there are so many evils to avoid or overcome that the task of election astrology is overwhelming. To some degree, that is true. Man is in a very bad position in the universe, but he is higher than the animals. In the instructional curriculum, we specialize in the teaching of the calculation of election charts.

Knowing how these charts work, and why they do so, is part of the learning curve. If you obtain a decent sidereal program and if you study this primer, that will bring you to the second octave of election competency.

Chapter Eleven

ESSENCE

Essence is different from personality. People in general are bewildered about this topic, even if they are aware of it. Carl Jung called false personality by the term persona. It is the external manifestation of what is known as ahankara, or false ego. In the natal chart, false ego is represented by the Sun. Sometimes, this is called the mind's ego. False ego is the subtlest manifestation of the astral body, a.k.a., the shukshma-sharira. False personality is totally dependent upon identification with the outside world; in Sanskrit, this outlook is called bahir-mukha.

The planets stamp their influences into and on this subtle body at the moment of first breath. Another component of the subtle body is the mind. Of course, the whole of the subtle body is invisible to almost all men. The mind is the most integral component of the astral body, and it consists of thinking, feeling, and willing, i.e., willing acceptance of the desire that was connected to an initial thought. The mind accepts or rejects thoughts based upon feelings connected to these thoughts. The mind may choose not to engage in the action indicated by thought and feeling. In that case, it wills in accordance with the counter-desire of aversion.

The mind is symbolized by the Moon. Indeed, the Moon determines an important component of spirit soul's root identification with the modes of material nature, viz., his essence. Another name for *essence* is the **_conditioned_ soul**. This will be discussed as we proceed.

Consciousness or awareness, which is even more subtle than the ego or the mind, was originally pure. However, it is now contaminated by identification with the three modes of material nature, viz., goodness, passion, and ignorance. It is represented by intelligence, although it is not actually identical to intelligence. Intelligence linked to the interest of the Supreme (the process of buddhi-yoga) is the means of extrication from the cycle of repeated birth and death in the material world.

The modes work in different mixtures in everyone. There are eighty-one categories of these; they work through the matrix of the subtle body as a whole. They especially work through the false ego, since it is the linchpin of contaminated consciousness. As just mentioned, there are eighty-one different varieties or combinations of any individual's essence in material contamination. The conditioned soul's entanglement in the wheel of reincarnation, the wheel of samsara, is based upon the backdrop of material desire. Desires are practically unlimited, but they are all a subtle form of conditioning of the soul in bondage. They are all intrinsically related to the aforementioned three modes of material nature.

We are on the Earth planet. Astrological lagna is calculated because of our situation on this planet, and lagna is the fulcrum of the horoscope. It (the ascendant) must therefore have a prominent effect on our essence, as well. Lagna indicates who we are in this incarnation.

Then we come to the Sun, which, as aforementioned, rules false ego. It will have, in many (but not all) cases another prominent effect on our essence. Our attitude or temperament in life is determined by the Moon, the lord of the mind. Mental attitudes are formed by intelligence, i.e., intellectual attitudes. The substance of mind most definitely has a direct relation to essence.

Then there is the most powerful planet in our natal chart, determined by accurate calculation of the shad-balas. It may also come into play in relation to essence, but that depends upon another factor, viz., if the Sun is weak or only mediocre in strength.

The lagna represents the conditioned self; it represents the physical body, as well. The gross physical body—what we can see and smell—is composed of earth, water, and fire. The subtler physical body—called the pranamaya-kosha in Sanskrit—is composed of air and ether. Finer than these is the aforementioned shukshma-sharira, the subtle body. At the moment of first breath, a specific degree and minute of sidereal arc is on the eastern horizon; this is the point of the ascendant. In relation to that point of lagna, we look to the lord of the dvadasamsha where that lagna point is located.

To summarize, these are the factors I look at in order to determine astrological essence: The lagna lord, the point of the ascendant, the Sun, the Moon, and, if the Sun is not at least somewhat strong or prominent in a person, the most powerful planet of the chart.

We look to the trimsamsha of the Sun, or, if he is weak (or even mediocre in strength), we look to the trimsamsha of the strongest planet in the chart. As such, one portfolio is either the Sun or the strongest planet in the chart, in terms of that planet's trimsamsha placement. The Sun is objectively (as per naisargika bala) the strongest planet in the chart. However, after shad-bala is calculated, he often does not remain the most powerful planet.

False ego is sometimes very weak in a chart. Such an individual does not wear his "persona" very well; in rare cases, he may even have dropped it more or less entirely. People with a weak or mediocre Sun also often have inferiority complexes. They do not get the benefit of having false personality act as a kind of shield to reflect so many influences coming into the subtle body. With them, "what you see is what you get." They have neither the inclination nor the power to project egoistic pretenses.

With them, you look to the trimsamsha of the most powerful planet instead of the Sun. "I am the doer" and "I am the enjoyer" are the two psychic dimensions of false ego. I consider this part of the astrological essence of any conditioned soul.

Until an elevated stage of spiritual life is attained, false ego itself functions as an integral part of a person's essence, despite the fact that it secondarily manifests as false personality—separate from essence. Proclivity towards purity, activity, or inertia is found according to the trimsamsha of the Sun *or* the trimsamsa of the strongest planet in the natal chart.

The mind is also a component of essence; the mind can be a friend or an enemy. The *attitude or temperament* of any individual is determined by the nakshatra of the Moon; this is in terms of its gana, which has been described in detail in the chapter on the Moon in the various nakshatras.

These are then two of the four components of a person's essence.

Obviously, as mentioned previously in this chapter, the ascendant must factor into determining a conditioned soul's essence. Indeed, as per my realization, point of lagna and the lord of lagna determine the other two components of this astrological calculation. As far as point of lagna is concerned, we look to the lord of the dvadasamsha where that point of the ascendant is situated.

So far, we have a trimsamsha represented already (of the Sun or the most powerful planet). We have a nakshatra represented (of the Moon), and we have dvadasamsha (of point of lagna) represented. What subdivision, then, of the lord of lagna should logically contribute the last component of the four influences that determine essence?

Let us consider *lagna lord's navamsha*. How could the navamsha subdivision not be represented in this essential calculation? There is no specific text where I have found this confirmed; it is based upon my personal realization in terms of philosophical analysis. However, there are four components that work together with the modes of nature to comprise the essence of a conditioned soul.

How do we know this? Vedic texts state there are eighty-one combinations of essence. The formula requires, on one side, four components; each of the components must then be in one of three categories. Those categories are obviously the aforementioned modes, viz., goodness, passion, or ignorance: three times three times three times three equals eighty-one. Obviously, a conditioned monad born with all four of these indicators in the mode of goodness will be like a brahmin, unless bad karma misdirects him in life on the platform of false personality. A person with all four indicators in the mode of ignorance would be a very dangerous criminal (a petty criminal if the planets and lagna were weak).

These four-for-four types are the exceptions. The majority of people—the overwhelming majority—have a mixed essence, but one of the modes is always predominant. Indeed, the only time you would have some difficulty discerning the dominant mode would be when two of the indicators were in one mode and the other two were in another different mode. In that situation, select the set that includes the nakshatra of the Moon as the prominent mode. *Your essence can be determined from your astrological chart.*

In the instructional course, we not only make this calculation for you but we explain it, as well. If your Sun or strongest planet is in the trimsamsha of Jupiter, that indicates the sattvic (goodness) mode for that component. If the lord of your ascendant is in a navamsha ruled by Mars, that indicates the tamasic (ignorant) mode; this last mentioned conjunction would be in connection with essence in terms of the physical body, like its blood, constituency, ratio of mucus to air and bile, etc.

I have given you enough here that you can figure out your situation, even at the level of octave two. It should become clear to you; it *can* be understood. Indeed, I am of the view that it *must* be understood in order to make occult advancement in life, and that this is one of the important contributions of sidereal astrology *now revealed for the first time*.

Speaking about essence *in terms of astrological levels*, there are five levels to this science. Octave one would include all that is bona fide in tropical astrology, as well as the first principles of Eastern astrology. Octave two is presented in this advanced primer. Octave three entails more details, along with the cultured ability to read yogas, determine your dashas, etc. This level would also upgrade and sometimes appear to contradict some of the preliminary principles previously learned.

Octave four can only be reached by a very qualified occultist possessing tremendous powers of almost computer-like memory. It has a similar relationship to octave three as that level has to octave two. The highest level, viz., octave five, is very different from the others. There is really no interpretation involved. Simply the revealed knowledge of the Brighu astrologers in North Indian (specifically, Hoshiarpur) or the sages who possess the Nadis in South India is given to you *as it is written*. That contact and revelation constitutes *the real essence* of this great science.

Chapter Twelve

LORDS OF THE CENTERS

Let us now confront the mystery of planetary lords in relation to our functions and mundane centers in the subtle body. Ouspensky said that there are four chief centers; he called them ordinary centers (as compared to higher centers). Upon closer analysis, however, we can discern seven such centers, along with their respective functions. These centers are (from lowest to highest) the instinctive center, the sexual center, the nourishment or digestive center, the emotional center (and this includes the power or moving center, as well as the ethical center), the speech center, the mental center, and the intellectual center. Ouspensky did briefly mention the sex center. There are seven major planets. So, if there are seven functions manifest in the physical body, might not the lords of those functions correspond to the lords of the "ordinary" centers that govern these seven functions? Certainly, this appears logical.

You may remember, in my opening chapter on method and scale, I mentioned that both logic and philosophical speculation (sankhya-yoga) are going to be employed, in a subsidiary fashion, in this treatise. This chapter represents that method more than the other chapters.

As spirit soul, we are within a physical body and a subtle body (astral body); both of them are made of matter. Aside from this existential fact, it gets a bit more complicated. Vedic scriptures (known in Sanskrit as shastras) state that air and ether are material energies. Everyone recognizes earth, water, and fire as material energies. Earth, water, and fire constitute the annamaya-kosha. The Sanskrit word anna means physical or gross food. The Sanskrit word kosha connotes a sheath or a covering. More subtle than this is the pranamaya-kosha. Prana refers to air, but we can deduce that ether is a component of this kosha, also.

More subtle than both is the sheath known as the manomaya-kosha. Mano (manah) refers to mind, which is one of the three components of the subtle body, along with intelligence and false ego.

Now, we have all heard of the chakras. Some teachers from India have come to the West and emphasized the importance of the chakras, especially those that allegedly teach or taught a form of kundalini-yoga. Some Westerners accept these teachers as gurus. The chakras are certainly not a part of the physical body (annamaya-kosha). They are said to cumulatively form the kundalini-chakra. This kundalini is very subtle and mysterious. If you employ a search engine and type in the word "chakras," you will discover a myriad of assertions, speculations, and proclamations. Concerning all of these, the only thing that you will find agreement on (in relation to all the opinions you will read) is that there are seven chief chakras. The Sanskrit names of these chakras are also universally accepted (muladhara, etc.). Some of these opinions will state that the chakras are very easy to see. When I first read this bold assertion, I was reminded of how one (now deceased) teacher of an international atheistic cult claimed that traveling around in your astral body was also not at all a very difficult thing to do—as easy as going to the local grocery store.

Do not be influenced by any of these soft-shoe shufflers. Realization of the chakras entails the development of great psychic or even mystic powers, what Ouspensky described as miraculous powers. Development of some psychic powers is commendable, of course. Full mystic power is like being the greatest hitter at the Major League level, and the basic development of psychic power is like being an average hitter in Single A ball.

In this age, searching out, finding, and recognizing a qualified brahmin is a rare attainment. A qualified brahmin is that pure and powerful occultist who has actually realized brahman (which is transcendental) while still here on Earth. This realization is very special. Real mystic powers actually begin developing after this realization. Just previous to realizing *Source* localized, an occultist, yogi, or transcendentalist has attained all of the mystic powers in full. As such, propaganda that the chakras are easily and naturally realized is extremely deceptive.

Concerning the number of the chief chakras, that does not mean that each of the chakras is ruled by one of the seven major planets. The chakras are progressively realized and developed—in terms of their full powers and benedictions—after brahman realization. Brahman realization, in the true sense of the term, is beyond avidya, the plane where the planets rule. It is counter-productive for progressive realization to assign planetary lordship to the chakras, but there is no doubt that the planets do affect and control our functions and "ordinary" centers in the lower sheaths.

Ouspensky used only a very few Sanskrit terms in his writing. I am not aware of his using the word "chakras" to describe the higher centers at any time. He instead used the word "centers" in two different contexts: Ordinary and higher. His goal, and the goal of his system, was freedom from material laws and the development of miraculous powers in an individual. In designating what he called *ordinary* centers, he was referring to those centers that exert mundane or ordinary control over the aforementioned functions. In relation to those centers, the higher centers are, more or less, in a dormant state — and he specifically spoke about them like that.

We should now re-focus on the functions and those "ordinary" centers. Calling them "ordinary" is, from my perspective, restrictive terminology. The term is too specific. The centers that govern the human functions in the conditional state are completely under the influence of the three modes of material nature: Goodness, passion, and ignorance. Other names for these modes are, respectively, normal, ordinary, and pathological.

By calling these centers ordinary, they are inadvertently limited (by this terminology) to the mode of passion. They may not be in that mode. Therefore, we shall refer to them simply as *mundane centers* here, distinguishing them (in this way) from the chakras. We shall sometimes refer to the chakras as *higher centers*. We shall be analyzing the mundane centers and their physical functions within this chapter.

The interrelationship between centers and higher centers is very mysterious, and there are conflicting opinions. Ouspensky, although he did not explicitly state it, indicated in his writings that the "ordinary" centers were separate from the higher centers. Most New Age or yogic group-think on this topic pushes the idea that they (the mundane centers and the higher centers) are, in effect, one — in other words, they are both in the same location. According to this line of thought, the "ordinary" centers *cover* the higher centers — and the goal is to purify the mundane centers in order to remove their covering influence.

Direct shastric references on this topic are sparse. There are *commentaries* that discuss it in considerable detail, but commentaries are not necessarily non-different from the truth of sacred text. Commentaries could easily turn out to be nothing more than opinion. Even worse, they could turn out to be misleading. We need more than that before we can confidently fix on any conceptions concerning the higher centers; we need sacred text.

In one sense, however, this part of the mystery does not need to be solved before we can take advantage of astrological knowledge relative to the functions and mundane centers. In Sanskrit, there is jnana and vijnana. These words are very common in Eastern spiritual circles. Jnana means knowledge. Vijnana means experienced or realized knowledge, i.e., wisdom.

Shastra (sacred text) and guru give us jnana. *Realizing* the locations of the centers and the higher centers (*if* they are differently situated in the pranamaya-kosha) requires a great deal of spiritual merit or spiritual advancement. Such vijnana is integral on the path toward the ultimate goal. Let us not, at this stage, quibble over the locations of those ultimate energy sources within the astral body. They will be realized in the advanced stage.

We *do* know the locations of the functions. We know that the mundane centers energize, influence, and control the functions. Let us, therefore, get a clear understanding of *this* dynamic.

There are five functions in the physical body. There are two functions in the subtle body: Mind and intelligence. There are mundane centers governing these functions in the conditioned state. Both the functions and the mundane or contaminated centers will have as their planetary lords one of the seven major planets; this is basic astrologic. That conclusion does not require astute occult discernment. It is just as fundamental that both the function and its mundane center will have the *same* astrological lord.

There are seven possible starting places, so let us begin in the middle. The *function* is *energy or power*. This energy or power is produced by the heart and lung complex, the cardio-pulmonary system. These two organs are situated in the same area and are very directly interrelated, as per their functions. Indeed, one cannot work (function) without the other. In order to move, you need power. As such, this complex can be considered the moving function. Now, can we deduce which planet is the lord of this function, and, therefore the lord of its mundane center? Is there shastra?

Fortunately, there *is* sacred text to help us make this deduction: *"The Self carries Himself two-fold: As life force (prana) and as the Sun."*

This is found in the Maitrayani Upanishad, 6.1. We all know the life force is the prana, and that the prana is situated in the lungs. The blood from the heart works integrally with the prana. As such, the lord of this center and function is clearly the Sun. The Sun is also the energy source in the universe, and it is the vital source in the physical body. We find a secondary verification; the color of blood is red, a color ruled by the Sun.

We now have logically deduced the lord of the fourth center, i.e., the Sun. Let us now start from the base and work our way upwards. The base of the higher centers is called the muladhara-chakra, of course. In the physical body, the correlated mundane center and physical system (function) is the excretory system. It consists of the large intestine, the rectum, the bladder, the kidneys, and the gland situated on top of the kidneys, the adrenals. This is an essential system, as the corrupt by-products of food and drink have to be eliminated from the physical body.

Which planet would govern this function and mundane center? Some opine that it should be Mars. They say this since adrenaline is secreted by the adrenals, producing the "fight or flight" reaction. However, *flight* is not a characteristic of Mars.

In Vedic literatures, the rectum is considered a place of pain; we all have practical experience. Which planet governs pain and sorrow? It is not difficult to deduce this lord: Saturn. Saturn is the lord of unclean places and things. The remnants of the excretory system fit this category.

After this, we proceed to the genitals. This is the place of (on occasion) intense material pleasure. In man, this complex also consists of the prostate gland. Semen collects there. This is the function of the sex center. So, which planet governs it?

Vedic astrology tells us that semen is ruled by Venus. Diseases in this area are called *venereal* diseases. The English *venereal* comes directly from the Latin for Venus. This planet is called shukra in Sanskrit, meaning semen. Venus clearly rules the reproductive function, as well as its center.

We then proceed to the nourishment or the digestive system. There's fire and related enzymes in there. There are pancreatic juices, gastric juices, insulin, and bile secretions from the gall bladder, etc. This system also consists of the small intestine. It is meant for disintegration. There are two fire planets in the astrological heavens: Sun and Mars. The Sun has already been assigned. There are two planets conducive to disintegration in the astrological heavens: Saturn and

Mars. Saturn has also already been assigned as the ruler of the first mundane center.

The pancreas is the chief gland here, and it is of an orange color—indeed, Mars itself is reddish-orange, and orange is ruled by Mars. We say that a person who is brave "has guts." Courage is a quality ruled by Mars. Mars rules this third function and its center as well.

We have already determined that Saturn rules the instinctive center and its accompanying function known as the excretory system. We have determined that Venus rules the sex center and the reproductive function. We have deduced that Mars rules the nourishment center and the digestive system. Previous to these determinations, we have discovered, through sacred text, that the Sun rules the moving center and the cardio-pulmonary system. The gland corresponding to this system is the thymus.

The heart is not only the functional representative of the moving center, it is also the functional representative of the emotional center. In material existence, we live in an ocean of emotions. The ocean of true love is also in the heart. For the overwhelming majority of people of this age, that ocean is covered. As such, this fourth or middle level (of the seven functions and centers) is where the moving center and emotional center operate.

Next we come to the larynx, but we are not going to consider the fifth center at this time. Instead, we are going to take a look at the sixth center, and, in doing so, we now proceed to the area of the brain. We have previously discussed the annamaya-kosha and the pranamaya-kosha. We now come to the manomaya-kosha and its sixth function and center, although the chakra governing it is not in the manomaya-kosha. The corresponding higher center is the ajna-chakra. *Ajna* means *command*. Mind makes *decisions*, because it is in charge of thinking, feeling, and *willing*. When you *will* something, you *decide* to do it. You then *command* your body to carry out that *decision*.

Indeed, the Sanskrit word *manah* (manomaya) means *mind*. And we also find Lord Shiva wearing the Moon on his forehead in the area known as the *psychic power command center*, a.k.a., the third eye. The most prominent impersonalist teacher from India, Swami Shivananda, also called this sixth center the manomaya-kosha. The most reknowned personalist spiritual master from India, His Divine Grace A.C. Bhaktivedanta Swami Prabhupada, confirmed that the mind is located in the brain. As such, we can logically conclude from all this substantial evidence that the Moon rules this function and center.

The associated gland is the pituitary, which is housed in the frontal part of the brain, just behind the nose. This general part of the brain is the psychic power center in humans. Mind means thinking, feeling, and willing. This entails sankalpa and vikalpa, accepting and rejecting—these are mental functions.

Thoughts stream into the mind. Then the mind has positive and/or negative feelings in connection to these thoughts. Sometimes the feelings that flow into the mind are conflicted. When either the positive or negative feeling eventually triumphs, then the mind wills to engage in the corresponding action. If the feeling is negative, then the mind engages (wills) an action corresponding to negation. The exact opposite applies if the positive feeling triumphs in the conflicted psychology.

That leaves two more centers: The intellectual center and the speech center. Let us first consider the seventh center, the intellectual center. Intelligence is called buddhi in Sanskrit. In every sidereal astrology manual or book that you may examine, you will read that Mercury is the planet ruling intelligence. In order to become an astrologer, Mercury must be strong and not afflicted. This is because considerable intelligence is required in order to be both an accurate and successful astrologer.

The primary Sanskrit name for Mercury is budha, and this word is very closely related to, and practically non-different from, buddhi or intelligence.

There is some argument that can be made to presuppose that the intellectual center is ruled by Jupiter, and I have considered that. For example, Jupiter is the karaka for the fifth house in astrology, the house of intelligence. Nevertheless, more powerful evidence is evinced when we hold Mercury up to the light as the ruler of this highest mundane center. Common sense, reason, and logic are required in order to make advancement in any subtle science. In this age, a man lives by his wits. It is important for any occultist that Mercury to be strong and without affliction.

Mundane memory is stored in the brain. There is a Sanskrit verse that says eating purified food produces finer tissues in the brain, conducive to better memory for accessing improved understanding. The pineal body or gland is located near the lower-central part of the brain; this is the gland connected to the seventh function. It is just

113

above the brain stem region where the spinal column connects with the brain.

There are two kinds of intelligence: Intelligence generated solely by the mundane brain and higher intelligence coming from *Source* localized. Mercury does not rule this last-mentioned intelligence, as it is directly ruled by *Source* localized. Mundane people who scoff at occultism have no common sense. They have not recognized their *other* intelligence—to think and do something different from the hackneyed routines of material life. They have no sense of reality. They have little or no spiritual knowledge. Any sane man can see the temporariness of the material world. Why waste time and energy by becoming more and more implicated in it? That is real intelligence. Common sense must be there in astrology, and higher intelligence, if it is present, can be helpful, as well.

If we come to a logical and astrological conclusion here, we shall conclude that Mercury rules the intellectual center. That leaves the speech center as the only remaining one and Jupiter as the only remaining planet to rule it. Is there any evidence for this correlation? Actually, there is: Jupiter rules the akasha or ether, the fifth gross element. Sound is carried in the ether and is produced by the vocal cords. We are considering the speech center here, and its relationship with Jupiter is tangible. Similarly, a teacher transmits knowledge to the student by speech; education is ruled by Jupiter.

Obviously, the logic and shastra used to establish the previous six lords—and their rule over specific functions and centers—left Jupiter as the only eligible planet to be lord of the fifth function and center. However, we are not limited to conclude this simply by that process of elimination; we have also produced evidence to supplement and verify it.

Returning to the subject of overall location, we know very well that all the systems in the body are intricately interconnected. The brain, in many ways, is the center for all the functions; from that perspective, they can all be considered to be in the brain. Functions cannot perform if the brain is severely damaged. Ultimately, deities controlling every one of these functions and centers are divine and occult personalities. They are within. Chaitya-guru, for example, is the immediate next-door neighbor of spirit soul, who is located in the heart. It is said that higher intelligence is also the next-door neighbor of spirit soul.

You have not been given *all* the answers in this chapter. Nevertheless, you have been given some good first steps and hints to eventually get there—knowledge that, in all likelihood, has never before been given in the English language, at least not in such a clear and organized format.

This knowledge has practical application. From a sidereal astrological perspective, you can determine from your horoscope—via the interpretations made elsewhere—what your strong and weak planets are. These will then correspond to the rulers of your functions and centers. In a crisis, you would then know whether to rely upon your instinctive center, your animal magnetism center (sex center), your courage center, your power center, your emotional center, your communication center, your mental center, or your intellectual center . . . or a combination of your best centers.

The functions are ruled by specific planets; I have conclusively detailed that. By accepting this knowledge (despite it being, in one sense, preliminary), you can make further research into the mystery of the chakras, the mundane centers, and the functions.

Astrological knowledge is not the same as transcendental or spiritual knowledge. Astrological knowledge is the highest material knowledge in the universe. Knowing how your fruitive being functions in the conditioned stage is helpful on the path toward ultimate realization. Knowing the lords of your functions and mundane centers forms part of that help.

> *yat-pada-pallava-yugam vinidhaya kumbha*
> *dvandve pranama-samaye sa ganadhirajah*
> *vighnan vihantum alam asya jagat-trayasya*
> *govindam adi-purusam tam aham bhajami*

Brahma-samhita 5.50

This is a Vedic mantra glorifying Lord Ganesha. Some say that Ganesh is the lord of the higher center known as the muladhara-chakra.

Chapter Thirteen

DECODING ALPHABET VALUES

The mysterious code hidden amongst letters of the Western alphabet, numbers, and astrological lords has now been broken, quite possibly for the first time in the West. Still, it is not accurate to call what I am presenting for the first time here a new system. Instead, I propose that this chapter constitutes the *discovery* of an ever-present system. Since this book is an astrological treatise, the relation of planets to numbers must also be presented in a table near the end of this chapter.

We live in a civilization where numbers and letters surround us. Our commerce is dependent upon them, as well as our calendar, our weather forecasts, and our financial well-being. Still, there is a mystery to them, especially when astrological correlations are considered. Now, *for the first time*, a detailed explanation of the numerological and astrological values of the letters of the Western alphabet is being explained.

You will find this presentation both accessible and sensible; it should attract your intelligence. It is absolutely logical, and that is part of my method. We are throwing light on the Western alphabet in terms of its permanent relationship with Sanskrit vowels and consonants. Sanskrit is the original language. You should be able to grasp the code with some intellectual acumen. If you deem it (decoding of the hidden relationship amongst the letters, numbers, and astrological lords) only esoteric theory, check your premises. We present practical applications. You can act upon any of them, usually without too much difficulty.

You do not need to wander around in a sea of mental speculation in order to take advantage of and fully understand this discovery. The system will change your ideas about numerology in relation to our Western alphabet. It is dynamic and will attract magnetic center. It will not take a great deal of brainpower in order to decode for yourself the actual values of the twenty-six letters of the Western alphabet we use every day.

The English alphabet does not lend itself at all to a phonetic numerological interpretation. For example, simply take our third letter ("c") from what was originally a Phoenician system. We can see (pun not intended) that it can be used to produce the sound "ka" or the sound "sa." Now, almost all English-speaking numerologists have assigned a very straightforward value to each of the alphabetical letters. You are probably aware of this system: A=1, B=2, C=3, D=4, E=5 . . . Z=26 (2+6=8). Simple.

Since it is based upon the current order of the alphabet, and not upon the varying sounds of those letters, there is a definite (although superficial) logic to it. Nevertheless, does this system actually, or accurately, represent the *root* numeric value of each letter of the alphabet? And would not that root value remain the value of the letter?

In other words, should we not question how the order of the modern and post-modern numerological system of the Western alphabet (originally Phoenician) came into being? Since our alphabet itself originated thousands of years ago, could the original order of letters existing before it—*and upon which it is based*—have been jumbled in such a way that the current order is haphazard?

We do not need to navigate through all the historical changes and missing pieces in order to answer these questions. The detailed evolution or devolution of our current alphabet does not need to be known. The questions can be answered very easily; we can skip the tedious work of what stages constituted the current alphabetical arrangement or order.

Every historian or linguist who is educated in the roots of modern languages knows very well that the English language traces back to Sanskrit. In analyzing the letters of the English language—in the context of the fifty-one chief Sanskrit letters (or simple combinations)—we can see evident correspondences. The only possible exception would be the last letter of the Western alphabet, the zed.

Our Western alphabet is not anything like hieroglyphics; the letters and all writing formed from them, have clear correspondences with Sanskrit letters. There is a similarity of sounds in most cases, also. This does not mean, however, that all of the basic principles of these two alphabets are synchronized. Far from it! As a matter of fact, one of the *most basic* principles is in conflict between the two of them.

In our English language, vowels accompanying consonants are treated as *separate* letters. There are also instances of separate vowels in Sanskrit. However, in Sanskrit, the letter representing a consonant *has the vowel already included in it,* as part of its pronunciation.

An abundant variety of examples could be given; I shall give just one. Let us take the seventh letter ("g") of the Western alphabet.

How do we pronounce this letter? We pronounce it as "jee." The letter itself is comprised of but one character. In its writing, however, a vowel (or vowels) would have to be added to it in order to display its pronunciation. As such, we cannot pronounce it as it is without adding (in this case) two vowels.

In other words, we have to use the tenth letter of the alphabet ("e") twice in order to represent this vowel in written form according to its pronunciation. This is not the case with the Sanskrit consonants. The corresponding Sanskrit letter (to our seventh letter) is automatically pronounced "ga," in Sanskrit, because the vowel sound of short "a" is already included.

For our seventh letter "g", we need three alphabetical characters to record its sound in written form. However, only one character of the Sanskrit alphabet is used to delineate the consonant *from which* our seventh letter ("g") has evolved (or actually devolved) over time.

Even though the consonants of Sanskrit are separate from the vowels, both the order and the sound of the Sanskrit consonants are uniform. A vowel, consisting of a short "a," is intrinsic to every character of each consonant itself—very much opposite and unlike the principle of what was the case thousands of years ago.

Nevertheless, a distinct relationship still remains between the letters of both the Sanskrit alphabet and the Western alphabet; it always has. That is going to be explored and explained in this chapter. What is going to be presented here *does* have an astrological component, and it's not difficult to see it.

We all know the current order of the English alphabet, but that is going to completely lose relevancy as we press on. What is going to replace it in importance is *the order of the Sanskrit alphabet.* How this figures into determining astrological and numerological correspondences will require intellectual effort on your part, particularly if you have had no exposure to Sanskrit. Not every Sanskrit character is relevant to this study; fifty-one letters do not translate into twenty-six Western characters.

Here are the Sanskrit letters we are going to consider: *a, short i, u, long i (pronounced "ee"), o, ka, ga, ca, ja ta, da, na, pa, ba, ma, ya, ra, la, va, sa, sa (with an "h" sound in it), ha,* and *ksha.*

Sanskrit alphabetical characters are divided into <u>nine</u> **basic divisions or categories. This is the <u>key</u>,** and it is very important. In the order in which any pronunciation guide presents them, they are:

1) vowels, 2) gutturals, 3) palatals, 4) cerebrals, 5) dentals, 6) labials, 7) semivowels, 8) sibilants, and *9) the aspirate.*

The aspirate is directly related to our eighth letter ("h").
We do not use dentals when we pronounce our twentieth letter ("t" or "tee"), our fourth letter ("d" or "dee"), or our fourteenth letter ("n" or "en"). We pronounce these as cerebrals. As such, the above-mentioned fifth category of Sanskrit alphabetical characters (dentals) is not part of any of the formulas.

All Western consonants are presented as alphabetical characters without any vowels attached to them. Each of them has a relation to a letter or character in Sanskrit, but that Sanskrit character (when a consonant) has a short "a" (pronounced "uh") *incorporated into its letter.* I'm going to continue to repeat this.

How we choose to enunciate the letters of our Western alphabet is often unrelated to the original correspondence. As such, determining the numeric value of any Western consonant is a rather simple affair: Take the value of the corresponding Sanskrit consonant and deduct a value of one (representing "a"); a simple formula leading to a self-evident fact.

The value of the first letter of our alphabet is one. The value of the first letter of the Sanskrit alphabet (also short "a," pronounced "uh") is one. This is basic numerology; nobody will dispute this. Every calculation thereafter (of the Western consonants, in particular) takes this basic rule into account. Indeed, there are only three identical and direct correspondences between the two alphabets; those are the only remaining letters not numerologically warped in the devolution from Sanskrit to English over time.

Let us now proceed to a delineation of the remaining correspondences. The first set of Sanskrit letters, having a value of one, are the short vowels: a, i, and u. They correspond directly with the exact same letters in our Western alphabet. Their value each equals one, also, because vowels come first in the Sanskrit language. When the Western letter "y" *is used as a vowel,* it also has a value of one. Two Western consonants also receive this value of one: k and g. They are derived from *gutturals* (minus the "a").

Sanskrit *gutturals,* being the second division or category of that alphabet, are valued at *two.* Since our Western letters k and g do not have the short "a" intrinsic to them (it has to be added), the formula for determining their numeric value is two minus one equals one.

Next we proceed to a *compound* vowel. The Sanskrit letter "e" is a combination of a and i. Both a and i are valued at one. As such, "e" in the Western alphabet equals a value of two: 1+ 1 = 2.

Similarly, there are two Western letters: "c" and "j". The Sanskrit consonant *ja* is a palatal; previously we have assigned all *palatals* a value of *three* (since they are the third division of that alphabet). In our Western alphabet, the consonant letter is detached from the vowel. As such, since that intrinsic vowel (not included in our consonants) has a value of one, the simple formula for "c" and "j" is three minus one equals two. The letter "c" also receives a final numeric value of two, as it is derived from a *palatal*.

This brings us to the English letters that have numeric values of three; one of these is the letter "o". It is a combination of e (value of two) and u (value of one) in the Sanskrit alphabet: The formula is two plus one equals three.

There are also three Western consonants that have a numeric value of three: "d", "n", and "t". We pronounce these letters as *cerebrals* (this was mentioned before). *Cerebrals* are the *fourth* division of Sanskrit. These Western letters ("d", "n", and "t"), unlike Sanskrit, do not have the short "a" intrinsic to them; their formula for a final numeric value is therefore four minus one equals three.

There are no Western letters receiving a numeric value of four; this is because we do not pronounce consonants as dentals.

Next come the Western letters receiving a numeric value of five. There are four of them: "b", "f", "m", and "p". They correspond to the *labials* minus the short "a" (intrinsic to Sanskrit consonants). The Western letter "f" is included due to its similarity to the Sanskrit *labial* pa. Both "f" and "p" are derived from the *labial pa*: The formula is six minus one equals five.

This brings us to Western letters with a numeric number of six. These are "l", "r", "v", "w", and "y". *The letter y is only valued at six when used as a consonant.* The formula here is seven minus one equals six. The letter "w" is included due to its similarity to the letter "v"; both of these letters came from the same source. That Sanskrit source is the *semivowels*.

That brings us to the Western letters receiving a final numeric value of seven. There are three of them: "q", "s", and "z". The letter q in our Western alphabet is a pronounced *combination* of "k" and "w", so we translate its value in terms of adding those two values, i.e., one plus six equals seven. The letter "s" is almost non-different from the chief sibilant in Sanskrit. As such, it receives a value of seven according to the formula eight minus one equals seven.

The *sibilants* are the *eighth* division of the Sanskrit alphabet. There are three Sanskrit sibilants, each with the same numeric value but all pronounced a bit differently. The last letter of our alphabet is very much like one of these Sanskrit sibilants. The zed ("z") is similar enough to one of these other sibilants (sa with an "h" sound), so it also receives a numeric value of seven via the same formula of eight minus one equals seven.

Finally, we arrive at Western letters valued at eight. There are two of them: "h" and "x". The formula for "h" is very straightforward. In Sanskrit, the same letter is known as the *aspirate*. It is the *ninth* division or category of the Sanskrit alphabet. However, the Western "h" does not have a short "a" intrinsic to it like the aspirate in Sanskrit. So, for the Western "h," its numerological formula is nine minus one equals eight.

The Western letter "x" has been derived from a basic Sanskrit character that is pronounced "ksha." This letter is often used in Sanskrit; for example, the warrior class is known as the *ksha*-triyas. This letter is one of the chief fifty-one characters of Sanskrit, but it appears to be a kind of combination of letters nevertheless. This Sanskrit letter is formed from a guttural (ka) combined with one of the three sibilants (sa, pronounced sha). However, the short "a," inclusive to *both* of these Sanskrit letters, is not present in the twenty-fourth letter ("x") of the Western alphabet. Therefore, a value of one has to be subtracted from *each* letter. As such, the formula for determining the Western alphabetical letter "x" is as follows: $(2-1) + (8-1) = 8$.

TABLE OF VALUES AND LORDS

Letter		Value		Lord
A		One		Sun
B		Five		Jupiter
C		Two		Moon
D		Three		Mars
E		Two		Moon
F		Five		Jupiter
G		One		Sun
H		Eight		Rahu
I		One		Sun
J		Two		Moon
K		One		Sun
L		Six		Venus
M		Five		Jupiter
N		Three		Mars
O		Three		Mars
P		Five		Jupiter
Q		Seven		Saturn
R		Six		Venus
S		Seven		Saturn
T		Three		Mars
U		One		Sun
V		Six		Venus
W		Six		Venus
X		Eight		Rahu
Y	as consonant	Six	as consonant	Venus
Z		Seven		Saturn

When our twenty-fifth letter "y" is used as a *vowel*, it has a value of *one*. Since we do not pronounce the consonants "d", "n", and "t" as dentals but rather as cerebrals, none of the characters of the West-

123

ern alphabet have a final numeric value of four. The Western alphabet has been formed from Sanskrit by being warped over thousands of years of cultural and literary changes. It has thus been completely broken away from an integral principle of Sanskrit, viz., the intrinsic inclusion (in all consonants) of the short "a" into the character and pronunciation. Nevertheless, every one of the Western letters can be—and has now been—traced back to *a part of* a corresponding Sanskrit letter.

It is the discovery of the occult principle—*that until now was hidden*—which is the apparent innovation here. Some examples of the astrological value of how this discovery can be used are as follows:

1) The initial name selection for a child,

2) Name changes for adults,

3) Adjusting a name in order to correlate it to a person's strongest planet,

4) Selection of a city for progressive development (the name of that city yielding a number that is favorable in a person's chart),

5) Selection of an unincorporated association or corporate names.

The basic principles of numerology—and the lords of the numbers—are not changed at all. What is changed (in most cases) is the final numeric value of the given Western letter. Every numerologist-cum-astrologer knows the principles, viz., you add up all numbers and then whittle them down until a single digit is at last attained. Each of those single digits has its corresponding astro-lord:

ONE	SUN
TWO	MOON
THREE	MARS
FOUR	MERCURY
FIVE	JUPITER
SIX	VENUS
SEVEN	SATURN
EIGHT	RAHU
NINE	KETU

The number four is not represented in the Table on page 123: Mercury is its ruler. Similarly, Ketu (south node of the Moon) is the ruler of the number nine. Even though number four and number nine are not represented in the comprehensive table, final sums of four and nine will be obtained, due to the abovementioned standard numerological process of achieving a single digit at the end.

Chapter Fourteen

YOGAS

There are hundreds of different yogas. Many combinations of planets are eligible to form a yoga; indeed, that is what the term means. All quality sidereal programs will delineate the *prominent* yogas present in your natal chart; only these core yogas deserve your full attention. Varahamihira in <u>Brihaj-jataka</u> presents numerous yogas in successive chapters, but most of them are variants of one root yoga. He also says that many of these yogas are only operative in the dasha or antardasha of one of the planets that comprise the yoga.

Let us first consider, in a concise fashion, the yogas known as raja yogas. Raja means king, but there are only a handful of actual kings on the planet today. Many millions of people have at least one raja yoga in their chart. Some persons in this age can become rich and powerful *like* kings of yore; this is how we should interpret contemporary raja yogas.

Varahamihira dedicates a whole chapter to raja yogas, but there are so many combinations and permutations of them possible that it would be taxing to list all of them in this small book teaching you sidereal astrology at the second octave. Most of these combinations are not present in the majority of people's horoscopes. Sometimes, four or five planets in specific signs and houses comprise raja yogas. The lords of a quadrant and a trine, together in any house or sign, produce a raja yoga. An exalted planet in a quadrant produces a mahapurush yoga, indicating great enjoyment.

The next consideration is what I call the cosmic yogas. In actuality, not all of them are benefic. There are no less than 1,800 of them; I'll merely list some of the more common ones, the simpler ones to recognize.

If all the planets are found solely in the moveable signs, that's one of these heavenly or cosmic yogas. If all the major planets are located in the fixed signs, that's another one. If all of the seven major planets are found in the common signs, that's a third variety of this yoga.

Nowhere in his book does Varahamihira describe yogas created by Rahu and Ketu. As mentioned hereinbefore, Rahu and Ketu are given very short shrift by him, and that is my perspective about the upagrahas, as well.

The influences of Rahu and Ketu are negative most of the time.

Although I agree with Varahamihira that the influences of Rahu and Ketu can be more easily overcome than the influences of the seven major planets, one yoga these upagrahas constitute deserves mentioning. It is called Kala Sarpa, and it is highly malefic. Obviously, since neither Rahu nor Ketu rule a dasha (contrary to the assertion of vimshottari), this Kala Sarpa Yoga is in effect for the duration of a person's life. It is formed when all the major planets are on one side of the perpetual opposition between Rahu and Ketu. It is arguably the most dreadful of negative yogas.

Returning to the cosmic or heavenly yogas, when all the planets reside in kendras, that is one. When all the benefics reside in kendras, that is a very good one. When all of the malefics reside in kendras, that is a very bad one—but those malefics do increase the influence of the chart. A malefic exalted is actually a benefic, so its placement in a quadrant must be read as a benefic in a kendra; it forms a mahapurush yoga. When all the planets are in trines (the first, the fifth, and ninth houses), that produces a heavenly yoga. When all the planets are situated outside the kendras, that is one. When all the planets are each in consecutive signs, that is a heavenly yoga.

What is interesting here is that everyone has at least one of these cosmic yogas, because every single possible combination is covered. For example, if all of your planets (excluding Rahu and Ketu) are in four signs—and these do not need to be consecutive signs—it is called Kedara Yoga. Those with this combination (not uncommon) do good for others. These specific yogas (all planets in one, two, three, four, five, six, or seven houses) are active throughout the duration of life.

Next, we consider yogas connected to Moon. Varahamihira dedicates a whole chapter to lunar yogas. What is interesting in that chapter is that two well-known yogas in this category—special but not rare—are not mentioned by him. I shall, however, mention them. One is known as Gaja-keshari Yoga. It is formed when Moon is conjoined Jupiter or when they aspect one another in opposition. Another similar lunar yoga is called Chandra-mangala Yoga. This is when Moon and Mars are either conjunct or in opposition (same arrangement as Gaja-keshari Yoga). Both of these yogas are highly propitious.

The most important lunar yogas, from my perspective, are divided into four categories: sunapha, anapha, dhurudhura, or kemadruma. Every individual has only one of these four lunar yogas active in his or her chart. This is how you determine them. First, notice the sign of the Moon. Next, eliminate the Sun from the mix, as it is never a part of this yoga. Now, look to the houses on each side of the Moon. Alone or in combination, do you find Mars, Mercury, Jupiter, Venus, and/or Saturn occupying one or both of these houses? If both the second and twelfth from the Moon are unoccupied, that is known as Kemadruma Yoga; it has a very unfavorable reading.

If only the second house from the Moon is occupied, that is called Sunapha Yoga. It has a favorable reading. If only the twelfth house is occupied, that is called Anapha Yoga. It also has a favorable reading. If both are occupied, that is called Durudhura Yoga. It has a highly favorable reading. What follows is a description of each of these four lunar yogas:

Sunapha: You acquire money by your own effort and are endowed with above-average intelligence, wealth, and fame.

Anapha: You possess influence and authority, are good-natured, healthy, famous, sensual, peaceful, and well-dressed.

Durudhura: You enjoy pleasures from your possessions, secure vehicles, obtain wealth, and acquire faithful servants.

Kemadruma: You are morose, mean, unclean, often miserable, and have a spontaneous tendency to be wicked.

Obviously, there will be counter-indicators to tendencies and traits in virtually every chart, so one yoga rarely tells the whole story. Still, each of these four lunar yogas constitutes an important influence.

Then there are ascetic yogas. In one sense, the rule for them is one, viz., the yoga is either obtained or is not activated as per that one rule. It is simple: At least four of the major planets must occupy one sign. The technical name for this yoga is Pravrajya Yoga. That chapter of Brihaj-jataka (on ascetic yogas) describes the many details connected to various combinations that constitute this yoga. The most powerful planet of the combination (remember, it can be four, five, six, or even seven planets in one sign) will determine what kind of ascetic order you will be attracted to or join.

Although few people have this yoga, Varahamihira's chapter on it even describes planetary alignments that indicate if you'll switch allegiance (from one cult or order to another) during your life. This Pravrajya Yoga chapter describes if you will attain initiation into the cult during your affiliation with it. The strongest planet of the yoga, or a lunar aspect on the sign constituting the yoga, determines this.

The last chapter where Varahamihira describes yogas deals with all seven major planets as per their placements in subdivisions (vargas). We have covered some of the technicalities of these vargas previously; they are further elucidated in Appendix Two. Any decent sidereal program will list these varga yogas. However, *many of those delineations will not be listed accurately*—indeed, most of them— because a person will not have an accurate ayanamsha programmed into his computations. Please review the essential importance of an accurate ayanamsha. Each of your planets was, in its universal situation at the time of your birth, located in a specific navamsha and a specific dvadasamsha. Incorrect placement in trimsamsha happens less often. An inaccurate placement in connection to navamsha and dvadasamsha is commonplace now, unfortunately. A very inaccurate ayanamsha will always miss the dvadasamsha and often will place the planet in a wrong navamsha, as well. The lagna point often will also be negatively impacted by an inaccurate ayanamsha.

In his chapter on varga yogas, Varahamihira describes the yoga created by an exalted planet conjunct a planet friendly to it. This varga yoga chapter also contains a description of yogas based upon sign placements; although the sign is technically not a subdivision, it is a subdivision of the zodiac.

The planets, in their various signs and houses, determine a conditioned soul's relationship with the modes of nature and the material world.

To reiterate, regurgitating a detailed description of all possible yogas in this treatise would easily double the size of this book. Let your sidereal program list them for you, and, hopefully, that listing will be comprehensive concerning the prominent ones. There usually will not be too many important yogas formed in any one chart; on average, a person often has less than a handful of important yogas.

Another option, if you are keenly interested in discovering all of your yogas, is to pick up a quality copy of the Brihaj-jataka and determine them for yourself. Aside from this option, there is a book by B.V. Raman called Three Hundred Combinations which can be consulted to advantage.

In the instructional course, where you will be taught the third octave of sidereal understanding, some details of the yogas in general—and your yogas in particular—will be discussed.

Unless you have some special power inherited from the past lifetime, it is, at least initially, difficult to recognize and interpret yogas. They are more complicated than reading planets in the signs. Being able to recognize them with accurate interpretations requires skill, insight, discipline, knowledge, and a sharp memory. That is why Mercury is considered a very important planet for astrologers. Mercury, the planet of intelligence, and Saturn, the planet of time, are the two most important planets for an astrologer.

I have shortened this chapter on yogas in this advanced primer, and that was an intentional decision. In the instructional course, I'll provide more access for you to utilize this knowledge for practical understanding. Nevertheless, it will require diligent work on your part. Sometimes, even advanced Western astrologers—with skill, experience, and excellent powers of memory—miss yogas that are right before their eyes. I have given you enough in this chapter to explore yogas on your own, if you so choose.

Chapter Fifteen

ASPECTS AND TRANSITS

The <u>Brihaj-jataka</u> presents one chapter on transits and a separate chapter on aspects a little later in the book. I choose to combine them in this chapter. One of the reasons I do so is that I personally pay little attention to them. There are many sidereal astrologers who would disagree with that perspective, but I say each to his own. I generally remain aware of the Moon's daily transits from one nakshatra to the next and from one tithi to the next. I remain aware of the Sun's transits from sign to sign, which happen in the middle of every calendar month. These are the transits that are most important to me. If transits and/or aspects are very important to you, do not allow my personal emphasis to affect your enthusiasm for making transits and aspects a major astro-study.

I am not creating a word-for-word or chapter-by-chapter translation of Varahamihira's work in my book. I cite and utilize his <u>Brihaj-jataka</u> extensively but not exclusively. As far as sidereal astrology itself is concerned, I am presenting an occult system based on his work. My system is presented in terms of how I have understood and how I apply his manuscript. I am not going to present all kinds of details that I do not use myself, that I do not consider essential, that I consider to be quite transcendable, and, in some cases, that I consider more or less irrelevant.

Another reason I do not emphasize transits is that I do not want to get mixed up with tropical astrology. Western astrologers put a heavy emphasis on transits and aspects, as you probably know. You could also do this as a sidereal astrologer, of course. It would be very time consuming. You could get some good, perhaps even spectacular results—but you would have to be willing to put in the time. As mentioned earlier in my book, aspects are essential to the tajjika system. That tajjika system is bona fide mostly in terms of the annual solar return chart, however. It is Vedic, but many of its rules do not roll over into natal or election charts.

The third reason I do not get heavily into aspects and transits is that studying them requires meticulous analysis. I am not a computer nerd nor am I an astrology freak. My brain is not always absorbed in astrological thought, although it is often absorbed in some form of occult thought. I devote significant time to sidereal astrology—this book is a testament to that—but not specifically to transits and aspects.

How much you want to absorb yourself in transits and aspects is a personal judgment call. People who can spend a couple hours per day analyzing all the angles, conjunctions, oppositions, and transits, from my perspective, may well be involved in the law of diminishing returns.

The process for determining transit results is called gochara. It is based upon a cumbersome (but not overly complicated) mathematical formula known as ashtaka-varga. The Sanskrit word *ashtaka* means *eight*. A planet is considered good (benefic dots) or bad (malefic lines) in transit through the various houses (signs) from its own position in the chart. This system also contributes different sets of benefic dots and malefic lines by each planet into each sign or house of transit. Each planet makes these contributions for its own transits and for every other planet in transit. There is also a set of benefic dots and malefic lines contributed from lagna. As such, the total contributions are from seven planets plus lagna; seven plus one equals eight, and that is how this method receives the name ashtaka-varga.

Vargas, as we have pointed out, are subdivisions—mostly, subdivisions of the sign. In gochara, the vargas refer to the benefic dots and malefic lines placed in the various *houses* of transit. I am not going to list these, because you can readily secure the ashtaka-varga details from many sidereal sources, including any genuine copy of Brihaj-jataka. However, even during that time, there appears to have been some controversy amongst those astrologers over just where some of these dots and lines should be placed.

In sidereal astrology, transits are considered as per their movement through the houses (same as signs), not solely in terms of their crossing the natal positions of other planets or the point of lagna. Where they cross natal positions is can also be considered part of the study of aspects. Besides considering the number of benefic or malefic dots in each house (sign), a planet transiting any house must also be considered in terms of how it functions in that sign. For example, say a transiting planet is going through a house where there are four benefic dots and four malefic lines. If that house is also its sign of exaltation, passage through it will be good.

Then there is vedha, which is another part of the meticulous analysis required here. Just to use one example, when the Sun transits

134

the third house from its natal position, that is often a good transit—since the Sun contributes a benefic dot there for itself. However, if there is a planet transiting another house that creates a vedha, even if that third house the Sun is transiting has six benefic dots, the transit will become adverse.

In Brihaj-jataka, Varahamihira only presents aspects in relation to the lagna, the Sun, and the Moon; the other planets are not even mentioned (in this connection) in his chapter on aspects. From my experience, the aspect of a malefic onto another planet makes that planet (receiving the aspect) more malefic or less benefic, but it does not affect the planet's strength.

When a benefic aspects an exalted planet, it makes that planet's greatness more accentuated. A malefic aspect on an exalted planet affects it negatively, but not that much. Planets exalted, in Mula Trikona, in vargottama, or in their own signs are affected less by negative aspects. Planets in friendly signs are more affected by a malefic aspect.

In comparison to weak planets, strong planets are less affected by negative aspects. When a benefic aspects a debilitated planet, it helps it a bit; it certainly does not make it a benefic, however. A powerful malefic aspecting a debilitated planet makes it significantly worse. Sign placement, house placement, and the rest of shad-bala are the most important calculations to determine a planet's power. The nakshatra of the Moon, and its reading as per that constellation, is also more important than the aspects it receives from various benefic or malefic planets.

Varahamihira mentions a special lunar feature or rule (and I have previously mentioned this rule) at the tail end of his chapter on aspects, although the rule really has nothing whatsoever to do with aspects. Perhaps this part of the text was grafted into that chapter some years after the first edition of his Brihaj-jataka. We have detailed the effects of the Moon as per his placement in the various signs. However, he might not show these effects (of the sign) at all. *If the lord of the navamsha where the Moon is situated is strong, then you read the effects of the Moon in the sign of his navamsha, as if that sign were his natal rashi.* Appendix Two shows the correlation between the navamsha subdivisions and the signs. At octave two of learning this sidereal science, loading up on all kinds of partial aspects—how they supposedly change and affect your chart—can get you myopically lost in the minutiae, fixated on some dubious trees rather than the forest.

Many of the sidereal astrologers I know only pay attention to the full aspects. All sidereal (Vedic) literatures present the same degrees of aspects for full, three-quarters, half, and one-quarter aspect effects by the seven major planets. Some of those are actually full aspects, even though generically they are not so (for the other planets). All planets give a full one-hundred eighty degree aspect. All planets give a three-quarter aspect to the fourth and eighth houses, but, for Mars, these are full aspects. All planets give a one-half aspect to the fifth and ninth houses, but, for Jupiter, these are full aspects. All planets give a one-quarter aspect to the third and tenth houses, but, for Saturn, these are full aspects. As such, full aspects are not merely comprised of one-hundred eighty degree aspects only for the major planets; the exception here is the Sun and the Moon, of course.

CONCLUSION

My advice is to forget all the post-modern astrological babble, sometimes disguised as sidereal science, because a great deal of it goes against basic Eastern teachings. The real and important details have been clarified in this book. You are not living a life that you cannot know about; indeed, you are meant to know how it is actually playing out. This flash lifespan is not only about you, because you are a dream body created by Maha Vishnu. As such, you are governed by intricate laws. You are not actually living your own dream; you are living the dream He has created for you in a human body within this cosmos. *Source* Universal, the Supreme Form of Time, is His direct representative in the material universe.

Sidereal astrology is the science of time. You do not need to remain unknown to yourself, as long as you actually want to understand everything that is governing the rare human form of life that you have now been granted. The human form is a special opportunity to escape the clutches of samsara or reincarnation, and an understanding of sidereal astrology helps you to achieve that. You can secure it by transcending the mundane influence of the planets through knowledge and detachment.

Let us briefly review the major theme of this book: Self-realization can be powerfully assisted by the occult science of sidereal astrology. You cannot completely depend upon others to do the work for you, but you *can* accept genuine facility and assistance when it is available. With this astrological knowledge, you can then make important decisions that otherwise could not have been definitively made; some of those decisions will be abortive.

Group-think is counterproductive to your real interests; genuine occultists never engage in it. Sidereal astrology is meant for a strong individual who insists upon bucking that devolutionary trend of this age. Any *individual* is usually a sane and rational being. However, in this age, put him or her within some kind of group, and he or she immediately becomes a blockhead.

This stark principle must become an integral part of your realization. There is no longer any need not be swayed by popular astro-opinion. You now can protect yourself from so many misconceptions about yourself simply by making a sincere and serious study of this book on the advanced primary considerations of the science.

Common-place teachings supposedly related to sidereal astrology have been jettisoned here, but *it is up to you* to discard them for yourself and act upon the knowledge as it is. There is a great deal of chaff embedded in the wheat of Western sidereal teachings; I have given you powerful hints on how to remove it. You can now learn the essence of this occult science and go on to more expansive realizations through the self-help program provided.

What is the use of an overload of details and information? They only serve to bog you down in endless conflicting interpretations, contradictions, and counter-indicators. There is no clear judgment to be obtained there; it does not constitute real advancement in the science. Securing clear astrological judgment is what is wanted, and that automatically helps you to transcend the influence of your bad karma.

Something is happening to you, and you need to know all about it. You can categorically know exactly what it is. You can know which influences are helpful and which are harmful to your material, occult, and spiritual objectives. You can know how to ward off adverse influences, and I give you some practical hints how to do so in this book. You can avoid the traps when you know how they are set and where they are located.

Your conditioning is primarily within you, and knowing how the planets reinforce it is essential knowledge for every genuine occultist and siderealist. Even at octave two, you can purchase many books that are much longer than this one,_and they will all, at least superficially, appear to be interesting reads.

However, if you sit back and analyze just what you actually got from them, you will clearly see that you secured little for your investment. In complete opposition to that, this book actually gives you something. C.O.R.E. Sidereal Astrology can also help by bringing you a notch up to the third octave; it packs a great deal of powerful knowledge in each segment of the curriculum. That knowledge is all tied together in a comprehensive system, free from contradiction, and that principle is applied in this book, as well. Why should volume even be an issue? It is quality that is important, not quantity.

This primer can be considered a preparatory study for the instructional or integrated occult studies course. That study will be a comprehensive course that utilizes sidereal astrology. It will teach you how to understand yourself, explaining the roots of all essential astrological topics in a personal and holistic way. In other words, you can take advantage of it as a follow-up course if you choose, and an opportunity for further metaphysical investigation. Few primers or books on astrology offer this; I know of none.

You are a spirit soul currently implicated in matter. I have presented this knowledge, regarding the principles and laws of your entanglement, in a clear and detailed manner. It has been presented in a somewhat basic fashion, because it is meant for second level understanding. It has been presented in terms of the planetary and sidereal influences, and it is a non-sectarian work. This knowledge, however, cannot be considered secular—not in the general sense of how that term is applied in the West.

For sidereal astrology to be genuine, there has to be realization of its connection to *Source* Universal, the Kala Purusha. He is separate from and far superior to you and me. When you become self-realized, you will not see yourself to be *Source* Universal. Materialistic, secular atheism and sidereal astrology do not go well together.

This primer is clear, direct, and simple. A system is presented in it, and that system has many practical implications and applications. For those who still consider the chrome on their car to be important, this book will have little or no value. For those who have rejected superficial values and who particularly relish compelling knowledge presented in a concentrated format, this book could be the Eureka! moment you have been waiting for.

You are now facing a metaphysical challenge, and you have turned your life around in order to secure some genuine answers. This knowledge was presented by Varahamihira in a neat little book many centuries ago, just for people like you and me at this time. We know the basic moral and ethical prerequisites, we have made some connection to Conscience, but we want to go further. We have a higher aim. We want to implement sidereal principles with ingenuity, intelligence, intuition, and a firm metaphysical footing. This system enables you to take control of your life in a way that accords with the *actual reason* the planets and stars were created in the first place.

This primer helps to lift you above all superficialities that trend in a wrong direction. It uplifts you from the whirlpool of disintegration toward integration. It acts as a springboard for further enlightenment, culminating in rejuvenation—at least in the preliminary stage. Ignorance is our great enemy, and Truth is our great friend.

This is an advanced primer, presented in a clear and concentrated way for the very first time in the English language. It is your opportunity to take advantage of sidereal astrology. Vijnana means wisdom. You become enlivened when your astrological decisions pan out. Sidereal astrology allows you to understand better how to obtain things and to avoid other things. Both wisdom and wealth serve as defenses. As Sean Connery said, money is hard to make and even harder to keep. Astrological wisdom, however, should be continuous once you have secured it. If you decide not to apply the principles presented here, you will not be able to realize what they could have delivered benefit; you can't prove a negative. However, if you become committed to its understanding and application, solid sidereal wisdom will now be yours.

Appendix One

1) **BIRTH NAMES AND NAME CHANGES.** Your birth time, birthplace, and date of birth are required, and *this is the case with all the other services*. You obviously retain the option to offer name suggestions, and I shall determine which of them I consider to be the most propitious. **Cost: $14.00.**

2) **ELECTION CALCULATIONS.** Include your desired time-frame for the election, and the nature of the initiative. If we cannot find a suitable election time, your charge will only be ten dollars. **Cost: $23.00 per election chart.**

3) **COMPATIBILITY CHART.** Two sets (time, place, date) of birth data must be submitted, of course. Then a lunar compatibility chart will be calculated, including specific interpretations, subdivision comparisons, and explanation of the essentials. A special relationship chart--explained according to each person's *solar* sign, navamsha, and declination--is also part of this reading. **Cost: $41.00.**

4) **BASIC NATAL CHART.** A *basic* description of your horoscope, in terms of the planets, signs, houses, benefics, malefics, neutral planets, and yogakaraka, (which may or may not be present). Only the prominent yogas will be discussed. Your essence will be described, along with favorable numbers, favorable dates, and favorable colors. Your occupational indicators will be explained astrologically and practically, along with some other *fundamentals*. **Cost: $45.00.**

5) **DETAILED NATAL CHART.** Everything from the basic natal, plus discussion of your prominent aspects. There will be an analysis dashas, along with a description of each of these life phases. Some secondary yogas will be analyzed, and other subtle significators will be discussed. **Cost: $79.00.**

6) **ASTROLOGICAL CERTIFICATION.** If you have come to the realization that **C.O.R.E. Sidereal Astrology** presents a system for becoming skilled in this science at the level of Octave Three, then you can qualify yourself to make it a profession by taking this hard-hitting, concentrated course of instruction. You have to be spiritually and astrologically quali-

fied for this opportunity, however. I only teach prospective students personally at my cabin; not over the phone or by e-mail or snail mail. This means that you must be prepared to rent a nearby motel room or have a camper. You will need a four-wheel drive vehicle, also. You must be a strict vegetarian and free from all intoxicating habits. You must have accepted all the knowledge in this primer; you must more or less know it in terms of the basics. You must at least be a henotheist (being a theist is preferable); I do not wish to instruct witches or warlocks. You must have previously taken advantage of some of the abovementioned services, especially the detailed natal chart, which I have to analyze to see if you can understand.

I am offering this course for **Cost: $500.00.**

Karma and destiny are interconnected, subtle, and profound subjects. Experienced wisdom can become spiritually progressive as well, once you realize the key to understanding and acting upon the knowledge of a horoscope. Astrological enlightenment entails the extinction of everything that obscures the science of sidereal reality. Desiring to transcend fragmentation in order to see the total picture unites all the particulars in the study of any chart. You want to see it uncolored by your own personal preferences and desires; you want to see it in detail as well as in its own pristine simplicity. Astrological study is meant to eliminate vague, aimless, and unclear thinking at their very roots, because this art is not supposed to be some kind of decorative embellishment. Master the art of living by mastering the sacred science of sidereal astrology. The subject is complex, but it is only made more so by harboring so many unnecessary complexities in your mind. Self-exploration goes hand-in-hand with the study of the sidereal science; follow a straight line to your objective.

Contact the author and astrologer:
J. K. Goodwin
375 S. Main, Suite 108
Moab, UT 84532
jerouldkielgoodwin@yahoo.com

Appendix Two

TABLES OF THE VARGA LORDS

List of Abbreviations

AR=Aries; TA=Taurus; GE=Gemini; CA=Cancer; LE=Leo; VI=Virgo; LI=Libra; SC=Scorpio; SA=Sagittarius; CP=Capricorn; AQ=Aquarius; PI=Pisces; Su=Sun; Mo=Moon; Ma=Mars; Me=Mercury; Ju=Jupiter; Ve=Venus; St=Saturn

Hora Table

Signs	AR	TA	GE	CA	LE	VI	LI	SC	SA	CP	AQ	PI
1 Hora	Su	Mo	Su	Mo	Su	Mo	Su	Mo	Su	Mo	Su	Mo
2 Hora	Mo	Su	Mo	Su	Mo	Su	Mo	Su	Mo	Su	Mo	Su

The first Hora is from 0-01 (zero degrees, one minute of arc) to 15-00

The second Hora is from 15-01 to 30-00 of sidereal arc in any given sign.

The rulers of each of these subdivisions in each sign are listed. The signs they represent are obvious: Sun represents Leo and Moon represents Cancer.

Dreskana Table

Signs	AR	TA	GE	CA	LE	VI	LI	SC	SA	CP	AQ	PI
1st	Ma	Ve	Me	Mo	Su	Me	Ve	Ma	Ju	St	St	Ju
	AR	TA	GE	CA	LE	VI	LI	SC	SA	CP	AQ	PI
2nd	Su	Me	Ve	Ma	Ju	St	St	Ju	Ma	Ve	Me	Mo
	LE	VI	LI	SC	SA	CP	AQ	PI	AR	TA	GE	CA
3rd	Ju	St	St	Ju	Ma	Ve	Me	Mo	Su	Me	Ve	Ma
	SA	CP	AQ	PI	AR	TA	GE	CA	LE	VI	LI	SC

143

Navamsha Table

Signs	AR; LE; SA	TA; VI; CP	GE; LI; AQ	CA; SC; PI
Degrees				
0-01	Ma	St	Ve	Mo
to 3-20	AR	CP	LI	CA
3-21	Ve	St	Ma	Su
to 6-40	TA	AQ	SC	LE
6-41	Me	Ju	Ju	Me
to 10	GE	PI	SA	VI
10-01	Mo	Ma	St	Ve
to 13-20	GA	AR	CP	LI
13-21	Su	Ve	St	Ma
to 16-40	LE	TA	AQ	SC
16-41	Me	Me	Ju	Ju
to 20	VI	GE	PI	SA
20-01	Ve	Mo	Ma	St
to 23-20	LI	GA	AR	CP
23-21	Ma	Su	Ve	St
to 26-40	SC	LE	TA	AQ
26-41	Ju	Me	Me	Ju
to 30-00	SA	VI	GE	PI

First navamsha ends at 3-20; second navamsha ends at 6-40; third navamsha ends at 10-00; fourth navamsha ends at 13-20; fifth navamsha ends at 16-40; sixth navamsha ends at 20-00; seventh navamsha ends at 23-20; eighth navamsha ends at 26-40; ninth ends at 30-00.

The planet and their sign correspondences are clearly listed for each sign and each division; the signs are grouped as fire, earth, air, and water.

Dvadasamsha Table

	AR	TA	GE	CA	LE	VI
0-01 to 2-30	Ma/AR	Ve/TA	Me/GE	Mo/CA	Su/LE	Me/VI
2-31 to 5-00	Ve/TA	Me/GE	Mo/CA	Su/LE	Me/VI	Ve/LI
5-01 to 7-30	Me/GE	Mo/CA	Su/LE	Me/VI	Ve/LI	Ma/SC
7-31 to 10	Mo/CA	Su/LE	Me/VI	Ve/LI	Ma/SC	Ju/SA
10-01 to 12-30	Su/LE	Me/VI	Ve/LI	Ma/SC	Ju/SA	St/CP
12-31 to 15	Me/VI	Ve/LI	Ma/SC	Ju/SA	St/CP	St/AQ
15-01 to 17-30	Ve LI	Ma/SC	Ju/SA	St/CP	St/AQ	Ju/PI
17-31 to 20	Ma/SC	Ju/SA	St/CP	St/AQ	Ju/PI	Ma/AR
20-01 to 22-30	Ju/SA	St/CP	St/AQ	Ju/PI	Ma/AR	Ve/TA
22-31 to 25	St/CP	St/AQ	Ju/PI	Ma/AR	Ve/TA	Me/GE
25-01 to 27-30	St/AQ	Ju/PI	Ma/AR	Ve/TA	Me/GE	Mo/CA
27-31 to 30	Ju/PI	Ma/AR	Ve/TA	Me/GE	Mo/CA	Su/LE

	LI	SG	SA	CP	AQ	PI
0-01 to 2-30	Ve/LI	Ma/SC	Ju/SA	St/CP	St/AQ	Ju/PI
2-31 to 5-00	Ma/SC	Ju/SA	St/CP	St/AQ	Ju/PI	Ma/AR
5-01 to 7-30	Ju/SA	St/CP	St/AQ	Ju/PI	Ma/AR	Ve/TA
7-31 to 10	St/CP	St/AQ	Ju/PI	Ma/AR	Ve/TA	Me/GE
10-01 to 12-30	St/AQ	Ju/PI	Ma/AR	Ve/TA	Me/GE	Mo/CA
12-31 to 15	Ju/PI	Ma/AR	Ve/TA	Me/GE	Mo/CA	Su/LE
15-01 to 17-30	Ma/AR	Ve/TA	Me/GE	Mo/CA	Su/LE	Me/VI
17-31 to 20	Ve/TA	Me/GE	Mo/CA	Su/LE	Me/VI	Ve/LI
20-01 to 22-30	Me/GE	Mo/CA	Su/LE	Me/VI	Ve/LI	Ma/SC
22-31 to 25	Mo/CA	Su/LE	Me/VI	Ve/LI	Ma/SC	Ju/SA
25-01 to 27-30	Su/LE	Me/VI	Ve/LI	Ma/SC	Ju/SA	St/CP
27-31 to 30	Me/VI	Ve/LI	Ma/SC	Ju/SA	St/CP	St/AQ

Trimsamsha Table

	0-01 to 5	5-01 to 10	10-01 to 18	18-01 to 25	25-01 to 30
ODD	Ma/AR	Sa/AQ	Ju/SA	Me/GE	Ve/LI

	0-01 to 5	5-01 to 12	12-01 to 20	20-01 to 25	25-01 to 30
EVEN	Ve/TA	Me/VI	Ju/PI	Sa/CP	Ma/SC

Signs of Exaltation/Debilitation

	Planet Exalted in	Debilitated in	Highest Degree
Sun	Aries	Libra	10
Moon	Taurus	Scorpio	3
Mars	Capricorn	Cancer	28
Mercury	Virgo	Pisces	15
Jupiter	Cancer	Capricorn	5
Venus	Pisces	Virgo	27
Saturn	Libra	Aries	20

Planetary Friendship and Enmity

Planets	Su	Mo	Ma	Me	Ju	Ve	St
Friends	Mo	Su	Su	Su	Su	Me	Me
	Ma	Me	Mo	Ve	Mo	St	Ve
	Ju		Ju		Ma		
Enemies	Ve		Me	Mo	Me	Su	Su
	St				Ve	Mo	Mo
							Ma
Neutrals	Me	Ma	Ve	Ma	St	Ma	Ju
		Ju	St	Ju		Ju	
		Ve		St			
		St					

Degrees of Combustion

Saturn is combust when he is within fifteen degrees of the Sun.

Jupiter is combust when he is within eleven degrees of the Sun.

Mars is combust when he is within seventeen degrees of the Sun.

Moon is combust when he is within one tithi of the Sun; another way of putting this is that Moon is combust within twelve degrees.

Mercury is combust within fourteen degrees of the Sun.

When Mercury is retrograde, he is combust within only twelve degrees.

Venus is combust within ten degrees of the Sun.

When Venus is retrograde, he is combust within eight degrees of the Sun.

Appendix Three

ON TEMPORARY AND PERMANENT RELATIONSHIPS

Table of Permanent Relationships

Planets	Su	Mo	Ma	Me	Ju	Ve	St
Friends	Mo	Su	Su	Su	Su	Me	Me
	Ma	Me	Mo	Ve	Mo	St	Ve
	Ju		Ju		Ma		
Enemies	Ve		Me	Mo	Me	Su	Su
	St				Ve	Mo	Mo
							Ma
Neutrals	Me	Ma	Ve	Ma	St	Ma	Ju
		Ju	St	Ju		Ju	
		Ve		St			
		St					

This is a duplication of a chart from Appendix Two on page 147; these are the permanent relationships between and amongst the planets. Besides these, there are also temporary relationships to consider; these are created circumstantially. You can employ either the permanent relationships or the temporary relationships in order to determine the shad-bala for each planet. Making the extra effort to ascertain the temporary relationship will yield more accurate results, however. The rule for temporary relationship is as follows: Planets that are in the second, third, fourth or tenth, eleventh or twelfth from a given planet are improved or made better in terms of the permanent relationship to that planet. Planets conjunct, in opposition, or in the fifth, sixth, eighth, or ninth from a given planet are made worse in terms of the permanent relationship to that planet.

For example, say a planet is a friend to another planet in the permanent relationship. However, that planet is in the sixth house from this planet. The permanent friendship is converted into a temporary neutrality by this house of occupation relationship. If they were enemies in their permanent relationship, then this temporary arrangement would have made them great enemies.

In other words, there are five different statuses (instead of three) in temporary relationships: Great friends, friends, neutrals, enemies, or great enemies. It should not be difficult to comprehend.

The Moon has no enemies but also only has two friends. Mercury is the son of the Moon; nevertheless, the Moon is inimical to Mercury. Mercury, however, remains a friend to his father, the Moon. Saturn is the son of Sun; nevertheless, the Sun is inimical to Saturn—and this is reciprocal. Jupiter and Saturn are the largest planets, and they are neutral to one another. The Sun, Mars, and Jupiter have the most friends, three apiece. Saturn has the most enemies, four.

Remember the formula for determining permanent friendship or enmity: The lords of the second, fourth, fifth, eighth, ninth, and twelfth from a planet's Mula Trikona sign, as well as the lord of the sign where that planet is exalted, are his permanent friends. All other places are inimical. If one place is friendly and the other is inimical, then that creates a neutral relationship.

Concerning the trimsamsha lordships, they balance the hora lordships, i.e., the hora lords are only Sun and Moon, and the trimsamsha lords are only the other five planets, viz., Mars, Mercury, Jupiter, Venus, and Saturn.

Sidereal astrology can help you, either directly or indirectly, in any action. An action is composed of many parts. The five components of an action are the place, the senses, the endeavor, the performer, and destiny (daiva). Let us take, as an example, a "simple" trip for provisions from the forest (mostly on a rough road) to a small village some miles away.

In this example, the vehicle, the environment, and the road conditions represent the place. This is composed of thousands of minute components, obviously. The senses need to be functioning properly and in good condition in order to ensure success in this action. The endeavor is the way that the trip is undertaken. If the tires were checked for proper inflation before the trip, that would be part of the endeavor.

The performer is the person or persons enacting all this, a conditioned soul (or souls) who embodies a specific combination of the modes of nature (sva-bhava). The more he is in the mode of goodness (sattva), the better his chances for success. Daiva is represented by *Source* localized, *Source* Universal, the three controlling Deities of the cosmos (Brahma, Vishnu, and Shiva), and, of course, all down-line demigods, represented by the planets and the stars. These all can and do influence destiny, although *Source* is the Superintendent with the final determination or sanction. So, all of these components of action are sharpened, understood, and improved by knowledge of sidereal timing, in accordance with the rules of election astrology.

As such, this science is, to some degree, a system of self-help; it improves your chances for success in almost any action. In writing this book, I am offering you this advantage. This advanced primer has also been written for spiritual seekers who want a genuine reference and an advanced introduction to sidereal astrology. It provides a concise overview of the major laws and principles found in the sidereal science, and it answers important questions.

It provides you a good and, even occasionally, an in-depth grasp of the essential values of this very old system, but it still keeps everything clear and simple (as simple as possible). Sidereal astrology certainly has the potential to be resurrected in this post-modern age and to be rejuvenated amongst an ever-increasing number of progressive occultists. You are amongst those who want to explore its teachings and see what its many principles and laws have to offer you in terms of your aim for individual success.

This advanced primer also serves as an introduction to a deeper instructional course, described in Appendix One. If this primer stimulates your interest—and you are inquisitive to learn more about your life—I have provided you ready access to proceed further.

Appendix Four

MORE ON THE CHAKRAS

In the <u>Bhagavat-purana</u>, Canto Ten, Chapter 87, Verse 18, we find the following verse:

udaram upasate ya rsi-vartmasu kurpa-drsah
parisara-paddhatim hrdayam arunayo daharam

"According to standard methods presented by learned sages, some worship *Source* in the abdominal chakra. The sages known as Arunis, however, worship *Source localized* in the heart chakra, a node difficult of perception from which all the (one hundred and one) nadis emanate."

The primary residence of *Source* localized, also referred to as Paramatma in sacred text, is in the heart chakra, i.e., the anahata-chakra. Some ashtanga-yogis concentrate on *Source* located in the manipura cakra, however; a form of *Source* is present in every chakra, but the primary residence of *Source* localized is as abovementioned.

The gross or visible physical body is made up of earth, water, and fire; this annamaya-kosha has a pumping heart as its center. From the heart come numerous arteries and veins, and blood circulates within these, keeping the physical body operational. Similarly, in the subtle pranamaya-kosha, composed of air and ether, is located the anahata-chakra, from which one hundred and one nadis, subtle veins of prana, circulate throughout. The pranamaya-kosha interpenetrates the gross body, and both bodies or sheaths have a degree of synchronicity, obviously.

This situation is confirmed in the <u>Vedanta-sutra</u>, but we can consult the Upanisads first for more effective understanding. The abovementioned sutras of <u>Vedanta</u> are concise aphorisms that require commentary (in bona fide disciplic succession) in order to be assimilated. However, in the <u>Chandogya-upanisad</u> we find the abovementioned situation confirmed in the Book Eight, Section Six, Verse Six:

satam caika ca hrdayasya nadyas
tasam murdhanam abhinihsrtaika
tayordhvam ayann amrtatvam eti
visvannanya utkramane bhavanti

"The prana channels (nadis) number one hundred and one, and they all emanate from the anahata-chakra. Of these, only the susumna-nadi reaches to the sahasrara-chakra, the brahma-randhra at the top of the head. By departing through this nadi, a yogi transcends death. The other one hundred nadis lead elsewhere to rebirth within the material universe."

The nadis are like veins, but they are not made of gross matter; they are channels of prana. They are subtle, obviously; nevertheless, they are not constituents of the astral or subtle body, the manomaya-kosha. According to sacred text, the chakras are not located in the astral body; they are instead located in the pranamaya-kosha, wherein air circulates.

Mars rules the third mundane center, or conditioned covering of the manipura-chakra, which is called in this treatise the nourishment center. However, this center—the chakra of which is located in the region of the abdomen—can also be called the power center. We have all heard that a person with martial spirit is said to "have guts."

The warrior is ruled by Mars (as well as the Sun), and Mars rules the mundane center associated with courage. As such, this center can also be called the domination center. Mars is a planet of destruction. Food is destroyed by the chewing process (also ruled by fire or Mars) and then further disintegrated in the nourishment center. Similarly, warriors seek to destroy their opponents in one way or another. In that way, they dominate over others, utilizing their courage (sometimes it is for the purpose of aggression rather than protection) in order to overlord those who do not "have guts" like they do.

On the body of *Source* Universal, it is declared in the above-mentioned Bhagavat-purana that Jupiter rules the region of the neck. The neck and the throat are related, further confirming that Jupiter rules the speech center, which functions from the area of the throat (larynx).

Made in the USA
Middletown, DE
28 June 2020

11368201R00097